£1·50

With be

G000068821

Solving the Strategy Delusion opens new windows for looking at realising strategy. It rewrites ingrained behavioural practices to fit today's extraordinary strategic challenges.

Fons Trompenaars
Co-author of *Riding the Waves of Culture* and
a Top-50 Most Influential Management Thinker

Don't even think of embarking on any strategic change effort without reading this book first! It demonstrates not only *why* conventional planning has become irrelevant but, importantly, *how* to see, feel, think, and act strategically in today's fast changing environment.

James Sutherland
Chief Executive Officer, Cricket Australia

You are about to read a book that gives a fascinating perspective on how it doesn't work *and* how it should in many organisations when it comes to strategic change! The examples discussed in *Solving the Strategy Delusion* on how people react to change or keep holding on to the status quo are very recognisable. But in today's landscape this is not sustainable. Dr Marc Stigter and Sir Cary Cooper explore how to bring new strategies to life and think beyond traditional practices and models. I highly recommend this book to all Forward Thinkers *and* Doers out there!

Rick Denekamp
Vice President, Trade & Commodity Finance, ING Bank, The Netherlands

Solving the Strategy Delusion is the ultimate why, what, how, who, and when of strategy realisation in the 21st century. It will inspire, energise and give you a foundation from which to make strategy truly happen.

Paul Baxter
Chief Executive and National Commander,
New Zealand Fire Service

Solving the Strategy Delusion is an outstanding reference for realising strategic change in today's complex environment.

Zeger Degraeve
Dean, Melbourne Business School
Dean, Faculty of Business and Economics,
The University of Melbourne

Dr Marc Stigter and Sir Cary Cooper are to be congratulated for highlighting the need for a more holistic view on strategy – to use an Australian colloquialism they call a spade a bloody shovel! I commend them for that. In today's fast changing environment, we are seduced to a world of short termism without proper regard for or a focus on the future. In such a world, strategy is more often than not relegated to an annual repetition of talkfests followed by a plethora of communications of various forms without action or progress. This book challenges conventional thinking and provides invaluable and practical insights that will enable the reader to mobilise their organisation in a manner that will enable them to realise distinctive strategies which will endure. Highly recommended!

Darryl McDonough
Former Chief Executive Partner, Clayton Utz, Australia

Don't be deluded that strategic planning leads to strategic thinking. If strategic changes are to be realized then this book is a must for those who want to make that happen!

Professor Philip Dewe
Birkbeck, University of London

Solving the Strategy Delusion hits at the very core of challenges that most organisations suffer from in the current era. Too many organisations continue to plod along with old-fashioned thinking even if the paradigms have changed dramatically around them. This pioneering book delves into the causes of such delusions which occur around the much-exploited term of strategy. The authors present a compelling in-depth, incisive, and to the point view based on their vast industry experience and decades of academic pursuit on the subject of strategy *and* organisational behaviour. This is a can't-put-down book and a must-read for all CEOs and executives wanting to make a real difference!

Sanjay Mathur
Vice President, India & ASEAN, Foseco at the Vesuvius Group

How do you unlock deep customer insights and realise distinctive strategies? How do you overcome organisational inertia and unleash productive energies? How do you mobilise people who can, know and want to realise strategic change? This remarkable book reveals answers to these questions and in essence shows how to truly strategise from the outside-in rather than inside-out – even for biased insiders.

Christian Overgaard
President, Danfoss China

This remarkable book is a survival guide for business leaders who have found the ground shifting quickly beneath their feet. But more than that it's a logical path forward showing us how to realise distinctive strategies by unlocking the energy of people within the organisation. It's clever and timely.

Tony Gillies
Editor in Chief, Australian Associated Press

Almost all organisations these days claim to have a 'strategy' – it would hardly be fashionable to not have one! But how many of these strategies are delusional, destroy value and organisations? Many – according to this original book from Dr Marc Stigter and Sir Cary Cooper, in which they outline cases where ingrained and delusional models of strategy were held on to, despite their shortcomings. They demonstrate how to avoid delusion and achieve strategic wisdom. Such wisdom means ditching most of the security blankets and conventions that managers and leaders still hang on to, even today, such as command and control, managing by the numbers and through stressed out workers. There are better ways and this book elaborates them!

Professor Stewart Clegg
University of Technology, Sydney

Solving the Strategy Delusion doesn't naively claim to provide all the 'answers' but instead serves as a practical guide for you to challenge the status quo and change the way you think, plan, and put into practice strategic change. This is a book you are going to want to keep with you.

Grant Rickard
Vice President, Systems Support – Europe, Middle East & Africa,
Oracle

If we look at ourselves honestly as leaders, we are too often drawn into the crisis of the day and avoid or neglect the challenge and opportunity of effective strategic change. Authors Stigter and Cooper cut through the noise and break down the process to offer keys in unlocking the power and productive energy of effective strategy; it's a must if your strategy is to avoid being another failed initiative!

Mick Crowe
Managing Director, G&S Engineering Services, Australia

Solving the Strategy Delusion is a refreshingly new perspective on strategy and strategic change. We are presented with a systematic questioning on how companies tackle strategy and change, create customer value, mobilise people and exercise leadership, through several types of delusions. These topics are then explored in a sensitive and pragmatic fashion. A 'must read' in the strategic management literature.

Rita Cunha
Associate Professor of Global Human Resource Management
Nova School of Business and Economics, Lisbon, Portugal

Strategy as we know it won't cut it anymore in today's environment. The authors take us through a compelling journey on how to survive. This book is relevant to anyone with a desire to realising strategic change enduringly!

Jonathan Sampson
Regional Director, Hays, Japan

Solving the Strategy Delusion

Mobilizing People and Realizing Distinctive Strategies

Marc Stigter
Critical Management Group, Australia

and

Cary L. Cooper
Lancaster University, UK

First published 2015 by
PALGRAVE MACMILLAN

Palgrave Macmillan in the UK is an imprint of Macmillan Publishers Limited, registered in England, company number 785998, of Houndmills, Basingstoke, Hampshire RG21 6XS.

Palgrave Macmillan in the US is a division of St Martin's Press LLC, 175 Fifth Avenue, New York, NY 10010.

Palgrave Macmillan is the global academic imprint of the above companies and has companies and representatives throughout the world.

Palgrave® and Macmillan® are registered trademarks in the United States, the United Kingdom, Europe and other countries

ISBN: 978–1–137–39467–5

This book is printed on paper suitable for recycling and made from fully managed and sustained forest sources. Logging, pulping and manufacturing processes are expected to conform to the environmental regulations of the country of origin.

A catalogue record for this book is available from the British Library.

Library of Congress Cataloging-in-Publication Data

Cooper, Cary L.
    Solving the Strategy Delusion: Mobilizing People and Realizing Distinctive Strategies/ Cary L. Cooper, Lancaster University, UK, Marc Stigter, Critical Management Group, Australia.
        pages cm
        ISBN 978–1–137–39467–5
        1. Organizational change. 2. Strategic planning. 3. Organizational behavior. 4. Employee motivation. I. Stigter, Marc. II. Title.
HD58.8.C6566 2015
658.3'14—dc23   2014029169

To Billy, Emile & Bibi. They know why.

(Marc)

To my grandchildren, Jai, Isabella, Skyla and Emme.
They are the future strategists!

(Cary)

Contents

List of Figures

Foreword

The day I became a global CEO I walked into the corporate boardroom at HQ, stepped straight out and vowed not to return. My approach to winning in business had always been outside-in, not inside-out. My preference was to be surrounded by samba, not suits. This wasn't about to change. The ideas that counted before and that have mattered since didn't come from sterile rooms in high towers. They came from the hustle of the organization's corridors, the bustle of the market, and – above all – from the heart and voice of the customer.

Creating and executing great strategy is not about talking and doing. It is about listening, sharing and acting, with a laser focus on inspiring people. In this penetrating book on strategic change, the authors uncover this idea and address it in the global age. Driving the line is what I have always believed and found to be true, time after time. Emotional connections are the road to victory in business, just as in life. Success lies in the ability to connect with people and win them to a cause worth fighting for. Inside, outside and across an organization, if people don't 'own' the direction in their hearts, it's headed south.

Strategic change is first about knowing when not to change. At Saatchi & Saatchi I made no changes to the leadership team for two years, preferring to back them and to focus massively on new language and purpose and inculcating this through the network. Only then could I make meaningful decisions about team selection. When organizational change *is* implemented its intellectual quotient (IQ) invariably flounders for lack of an emotional quotient (EQ). As a platform, this book expertly maps the deluded terrain of organizational strategy. Too often the approach is anchored in the past, and tied to inward-looking and incremental moves that fail to engage the multiple audiences. Strategy that works, as the authors show, is as much about sensing as thinking.

Equally, it is about unleashing and inspiring people, not commanding and controlling. Revolution begins with language. CEO means Chief Excitement Officer! Language drives purpose, which creates belief, belonging and direction. Great change comes from burning purpose and a commitment from everyone to passionately pursue that purpose.

As Stigter and Cooper say, making strategic change happen is truly a people's game. They expertly bring to the forefront the ingredients of co-creating a compelling story and, of critical importance, explore meaning-making down to the level of the individual. In any change initiative, the individuals must desire the transformation. Why do people withdraw their energies? What flips an employee into overdrive in a vehicle of change? What must we know about sustaining organizational energy? The answers are here.

To IQ and EQ next add TQ, a technological component. The need to expand perceptions and captivate audiences gathers force in the technological and digital age. Today the constituents of any initiative to create value – commercial or social or political – have astonishing power to assess, engage or disengage. It happens at velocity. We live in an always-on, impulse-led, instant Age of Now. It's a high-speed connected time where a winning strategy is centred in creating a culture where the production line churns out one thing, day after day, ideas. Creativity has unreasonable power. It has magical power. It has talking power through a digital megaphone.

Solving the Strategy Delusion is right on this curve. The book will matter to anyone wanting to implement strategy because it intelligently explores how to see, feel, think, plan and act *differently*. I like how the work drives into the win zone of having ideas, insights, intuition, and involvement on all sides. Importantly, it takes us through the co-creating dimension of strategy. We live in a VUCA world, and collaboration busts the dam of volatility, uncertainty, complexity and ambiguity. As production goes hi-tech in an automated future, the winning cultures will be free flowing, collaborative and take in multiple perspectives, including the ones the authors call internal insiders, mavericks. We know from Stephen Jay Gould's theory of evolutionary biology called Punctuated Equilibrium that change comes from the edge of the species. The Age of the Idea belongs to the outlanders, rebels and rule breakers. Bring back the mavericks, say Stigter and Cooper. Organizations that compete on the choppy seas ahead must roll out that cool Steve Jobs line: Why join the navy if you can be a pirate?

To the IQ + EQ + TQ value equation, I would add BQ (bloody quick!). It's not enough to get things done; a great strategy makes things happen. Execution is the killer app, and Stigter and Cooper show us the critical link between strategy and execution. The right questions are addressed in this book, including: Why does execution fail? What is the role of middle managers in change? How to change engines while flying the plane? To realize strategy through individual action, what simple questions do employees need to answer?

Solving the Strategy Delusion is a comprehensive and insightful remedy for the field of strategic change, and advances the subject in original ways. Everyone working at senior levels of business and policy should read this book. This is a fresh and decisive contribution to the canon of strategy.

Kevin Roberts
CEO Worldwide, Saatchi & Saatchi

Acknowledgements

Marc Stigter: First and foremost, I would like to thank my friend and co-writer Sir Cary Cooper. I met Cary when I defended my PhD research and Cary was one of the examiners. It's been such an honour to be on the same-side-of-the-table on this occasion.

Many people have contributed unconditionally to my thinking over the years. They helped me to see, feel and think differently about strategy and organizational life. In particular, I wanted to thank Clarence Da Gama Pinto, Andrew Grant, Andrew Larratt, Brian Sands, Steve Taylor, Iain Everingham, and Jeroen van der Veer.

Thanks are also due to two special people with whom I have been on an intellectual journey for more than a decade. The wisdom and friendship received from Professor Caroline Gatrell and Dr Sharon Turnbull have been invaluable.

Thank you deeply to my father, Robert, who, during a formative stage in my life, supported me through various studies abroad. As a result of his encouragement, a thirst for lifelong learning was instilled in me.

Cary L. Cooper: I would like to thank all my post graduate, PhD students and those I have examined like Marc, who have worked with and developed me as a person and academic. Their contribution to my work has been enormous, and like any family are an integral part of my academic development, my second family!

About the Authors

Marc Stigter is an international strategist who works with organizations on unlocking deep insights and realizing distinctive strategies. His own insights have been gained as a global practitioner at executive level, as a research academic at doctoral level, and as a strategy advisor at organizational level. Marc is an Honorary Senior Fellow at the University of Melbourne's Graduate School of Business and Economics, and an Associate Director at Melbourne Business School. He has held executive positions with blue-chip companies around the world and currently is the Principal of the Critical Management Group.

Sir Cary L. Cooper is Distinguished Professor of Organizational Psychology and Health at Lancaster University, UK. He is Chair of the Academy of Social Sciences, the Editor-in-Chief of the scholarly journal *Stress and Health* and the author of many books on workplace health. Sir Cary received a CBE in 2001 for his contributions to occupational safety and health, and is a regular contributor to radio and TV on topics in occupational psychology and health. In 2014, Sir Cary was awarded a knighthood in the Queen's Birthday Honour's List for his services to the social sciences.

1
What's Going On?

Let's not beat about the bush. Most of our strategic change efforts aren't being realized successfully. Most of our leaders aren't consumed with organizational strategy but are instead overwhelmed with managing day-to-day operational challenges. Most organizational leaders don't have a longer-term strategic focus but are overridden by short-term performance requirements from shareholders and analysts. Most of our strategies aren't distinctive and created from the Outside-In but rather from the Inside-Out based on current resources and capabilities. Most of our organizations aren't really customer centric but are mainly sales and marketing driven. Most of our workforces aren't engaged but are paralysed by inertia and collectively withdrawing extra-energies. Most of our values and desired behaviours aren't being demonstrated consistently and enduringly throughout our organizations today. What's going on?

Simply put we believe that many organizations are trapped in deluded beliefs in relation to strategy. *Delusion* can be defined as a rigid system of beliefs with which we are preoccupied and to which we firmly hold despite the logical absurdity of the beliefs and a lack of supporting evidence.[1] It is rigid and embedded delusions that are holding back many of our organizations today.

In this chapter we focus on typical *strategic* delusions relating to embedded beliefs about Change, Planning, Leadership, Customers, People, and Behaviours as illustrated in Figure 1.1. We raise provocative questions in this opening chapter that are further explored and tackled throughout the book. We use the terms 'strategy', 'change', 'strategic change', and 'organizational change' loosely and interchangeably.

Figure 1.1   Six typical organizational delusions related to strategy

The Change delusion

Stating that strategic change is difficult to realize is not the point. We all know that. We only need to look within our own organizations to acknowledge the challenges in making change happen consistently and sustainably. If still in doubt we always can refer to John Kotter and other academics to tell us that between 70 and 90 per cent of strategic change initiatives fail.[2]

But how can such failure rates be endured? The short and simple answer is they can't. Isn't it incredible that even prominent organizations, let alone whole industries, are caught out, replaced, or destroyed without being able to manage the inevitably required strategic change? How can it be that a renowned organization goes from 50 per cent global market share domination in one year to just 3 per cent share within four years? Or, how can it be that another company enjoys a 20 per cent global market share when voted the fastest growing company in the world by *Fortune* magazine only for its market share to drop to below 1 per cent four years later?

Unfortunately, these are real examples as illustrated in Table 1.1 and the frightening thing is that our list could be endless. Are many of our organizations 'deluded' when it comes to acting on strategic change? We provocatively would argue: YES! So, what's going on? There obviously are numerous reasons as to why we often fail to realize strategic change. These will be explored throughout this book. But to start with one underlying reason for failure is that we keep holding on.

Holding on to the nut

Hopefully it's not stretching the analogy but it is like a monkey holding on to a nut. There is a YouTube video in which a tribesman somewhere in Africa can be seen catching a monkey.[3] A hole has been dug into the ground with an opening slightly larger than a monkey's hand. A peanut has been placed in the hole and the tribesman can be seen hiding behind a bush. Suddenly a monkey arrives reaching his hand into the hole, grabbing the peanut and making a fist with his paw. Now the monkey's dilemma: the monkey can't get his hand out of the hole unless he drops the nut. The neck of the hole is not wide enough. Of course, the monkey could drop the nut and easily get his hand out. But he won't. Despite having at his command the means to escape he doesn't but keeps holding on to the nut while the hunter walks up to the monkey and captures him.

We tend to do the same in organizational life. 'When a company is really busy holding on to what it has built, it is difficult to put enough of a push towards something so drastically new and engender urgency in it', as admitted by Frank Nuovo, who was the former Chief of Design at Nokia.[4] The ramifications of holding on can be dramatic for companies and some examples are illustrated in Table 1.1.

But many of our own organizations also fail to realize strategic change because of the monkey-trap. We focus on holding on to incremental improvement of existing strategies and offerings. We are busy coming up with new versions of old strategies rather than aggressively seeking disruptive strategic change. 'I look back and I think Nokia was just a very big company that started to maintain its position more than innovate for new opportunities,' Nuovo says.

Within our own organizations we also have a tendency to hold on, maintain our position, and look for opportunities from the

Table 1.1 Common examples of holding on to ingrained offerings and business models[5]

	From	To	Cause? Holding on to:
Kodak	Revenues peaking at $16 billion in 1996 and profits at $2.5 billion in 1999	Filing for bankruptcy protection in 2012	Their film & camera business even after digital products were reshaping the market
Blockbuster	60,000 employees & 9,000 stores in 2004	Filing for bankruptcy in 2010	Their perceived reliance on a brick-and-mortar model
The NY Times	Paying US$1.1billion for The Boston Globe in 1993	Selling it for only US$70million in 2013	Their conventional news and print model even after the rise of the internet and digital news
Nokia	50% global market share domination in 2007	Just 3% global market share and selling-off the company in 2013	Producing high-quality hardware and underestimating the importance of 3rd software applications to smart-phone offer
BlackBerry	20% global market share in 2009	Below 1% global market share in 2013	Producing phones with full keyboards even after users preferring touch-screens for improved navigation & viewing
Dell	Global PC market leader from 2003 to 2007	Going private in 2013 after 25 years trading as a public company	Manufacturing computers at ever-lower costs even after the dramatic rise of software driven smart phones and tablets

Inside-Out rather than the Outside-In. We become trapped within an internally driven paradigm where we look at 'opportunities' based on current product offerings, resources, and capabilities. We start to believe that strategic change is a response and not an anticipation. Strategic change becomes reactive by thinking from the Inside-Out instead of proactive by sensing from the Outside-In. We subsequently come up with indistinctive strategies and offerings. Then suddenly one day we realize with amazement that things are no longer what they were.

Holding on to ingrained models

So, why did, or still do, renowned companies as illustrated in Table 1.1 face strategic change constraints in the digital age? Why don't they capture the opportunities of today's and tomorrow's global economy?

The short answer is that even the best of today's companies together with most of our own organizations are holding on to an organizing model designed for an earlier era.[6] The way we still lead and organize our companies together with the way we strategically think and act is based on a twentieth-century model. We are busy holding on to ingrained organizing models unsuitable for managing today's complexities and opportunities.

Trying to run a company in the twenty-first century with an organizing model designed for the twentieth century places limits on how well a company performs or even survives. 'It also creates massive, unnecessary, unproductive complexity – a condition that frustrates workers and wastes money. The plagues of the modern company are hard-to-manage workforce structures, thick silo walls, confusing matrix structures, e-mail overload, and undoable jobs'.[7] So, we shouldn't be surprised that most of our companies still earn profits per employee at close to the same low levels earned in the past century.[8] We simply haven't become very adept at mobilizing our organizations and people for strategic change in the twenty-first century. Instead we continue holding on.

The Planning delusion

If we dropped into a boardroom or executive team discussion chances are that the relevance of strategic planning is being debated. There is an argument going on that strategic planning has become irrelevant in today's volatile and fast changing environment. The speed of the new economy has caused many executives to think that longer-term strategic planning is becoming immaterial.

But let's be careful not to throw the baby out with the bathwater. The need for enduring and distinctive strategies is actually higher in a fast-changing world. The reality is that creating distinctive strategies takes time. The fabled Eureka moments may lead to a novel tactical breakthrough but they rarely lead to distinctive strategic offerings. Strategic breakthroughs come from long-term and iterative strategic sensing, strategic creation, and strategic realization.

So, whilst strategic planning – as we know it – has become irrelevant it would be a delusion to think that our ability to create and execute distinctive strategies has lost any relevance in today's fast-changing world. Unfortunately, we often confuse strategic planning with strategy creation. We often seem consumed with the *process* of putting together a strategic plan as opposed to the *practice* of strategizing. Let's examine this further.

In search of distinctive strategies

It is not uncommon that once a year the executive team of an organization takes off to a retreat for a two-day strategic planning workshop. The output of such workshops tends to be a plan around strategic objectives that often have been developed during the workshop. Such plans typically include *financial* objectives like increasing revenue and net income by x per cent within x years; *customer* objectives like growing market share by x per cent through geographical expansion or the launch of a new product; *internal support* objectives like rolling-out a new IT (information technology) system within a certain period of time; and *people* objectives like recruiting and retaining the best employees who are skilled, motivated, and engaged.

Obviously these examples are overly simplified for the purpose of this discussion. Even so many of us will recognize similarly developed objectives. At first glance the described objectives seem balanced, from various perspectives and quantifiable. But to us the above objectives exemplify the many problems associated with developing strategies. Many developed strategies, like our examples, are mediocre and not distinctive. The mentioned objectives do little more than restate obvious aims. They provide no help to anybody within any given organization because they are just another common way of defining the universal objectives of basically all organizations.

The objectives in our example are indistinctive because they have been created from an internal (executive team's) perspective. Our customers couldn't care less about us wanting to increase market share. Our people all understand that we want them motivated and engaged because that means higher productivity and performance. But these so-called objectives are at best ultimate outcomes. What is much more difficult to try and create are underlying objectives from true customer or people perspectives. So, the real question to ask is what the underlying objectives should be that encapsulate value propositions to our customers or people. What are distinct strategic offerings we need to focus on going forward that are of true meaning to our customers (and therefore ultimately result in increased market share) or that are of true meaning to our people (and therefore ultimately result in increased retention, motivation, and engagement)?

Beyond periodic and monopolized planning

Strategy has become a tick-the-box exercise where mainly leaders focus on the planning aspect of it during an annual planning workshop. How can we seriously expect for deep insights to be unlocked and distinctive strategies to be created during a ceremonial planning session once or twice a year? And how can we assume that distinctive strategies could be formulated not only periodically but mainly by the leadership team? As though there are only a few selected people in an organization who can 'see the future'?

Again, we are holding on to conventional planning processes that are futile in today's rapidly changing and competitive world. But there is an urgent need to break the old habits of monopolized and periodic planning: those that don't simply won't survive.

Beyond strategic thinking

Breaking old habits of periodic and monopolized strategic planning is not enough. Distinctive strategies aren't created through conventional strategic *thinking*. It is obvious that change is constant but what is less obvious is that today's change is often non-linear. In other words, today's dynamic environment defies linear and accustomed ways of thinking. Strategic thought that mainly seeks hard, fact-based, and logical information may have been sufficient in the past but not anymore.

We now require distinctive strategies that originate in insights beyond the reach of conventional thinking. Deep insights are critical because they help us uncover true customer value and help us create points of differentiation. They help us understand the fundamental drivers of our business and challenge assumptions about our existing value propositions. So, a new strategic sensing capability is required that can help us discover such insights. It won't just happen by holding on to conventional strategic thinking nor can it be done in a few scheduled strategic planning meetings. Now that would be a delusion.

Beyond communication

Executive teams invest a lot of time on 'communicating' the developed strategic plan typically through bulk e-mails, on web sites, in newsletters, through town-hall meetings, or 'road shows'. But it's a delusion to think that proposed strategic change would become meaningful in this way.

There are major problems with this conventional 'communication' approach. To start with, and let's be honest, corporate strategy 'communication' is largely perceived as a one-way information exercise. Providing top-down information about what needs to be done is obviously easier than inviting a wide range of reactions and interpretations. But just informing people about the intended organizational strategy doesn't mean it's meaningful to them. True meaning for people occurs only through dialogue and sensemaking of a wider and compelling 'story'. Not just a PowerPoint presentation of yet again another strategic plan. And with an average of more than 200 emails a day employees are likely to quickly overlook program emails and 'boring' newsletters.[9] Also, let's not expect too much of the executive town-hall presentations with a handful of polite questions from the audience thrown-in at the end.

Rather than selling a strategy through conventional communication why don't most executives engage through deeper dialogue and sensemaking? And by interacting in a variety of ways that are meaningful to growing number of employees.

Within 'the next decade Millennials or Generation Y will make up the majority of the workforce. This generation is expected to have different behaviours, values and attitudes as a response to the technological and economic implications of the internet. They are history's first 'always connected' generation, and to engage them, employers will need to rethink communication strategies accordingly'.[10] In other words, 'texting, tweeting, blogging, tagging, posting videos and uploading photos are the mainstream methods for communication in today's society'.[11] If these elements aren't included in our strategic change management we've likely limited the reach of our efforts and the impact of our desired organizational change.[12]

The Behavioural delusion

The *values* delusion has swept through the corporate world like chicken pox through a kindergarten class. We are all aware of the motherhood-and-apple-pie values that appear in so many values statements like integrity, respect, excellence, and innovation. 'Most values statements are bland, toothless, or just plain dishonest. And far from being harmless as some executives may assume, they're often highly destructive. Empty values statements create cynical and dispirited employees, alienate customers, and undermine leadership credibility'.[13] Today we all are aware of the values delusion.

Another delusion that needs highlighting and closely related to values is around behaviours and performance. Within most of our organizations we put an equal value on demonstrating desired behaviours *and* on high performance. But the point that we provocatively are making is that high performers who misbehave are too often being tolerated within our organizations.

Through our research we found a mismatch between what executives say in theory and how they act in practice. Our finding is that many organizational leaders continue to hold on to high performers who consistently fail to demonstrate desired behaviours.

The matrix as illustrated in Figure 1.2 was adapted from Jack Welch, who labels the horizontal axis as 'culture'. For the sake of

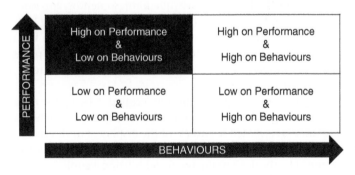

Figure 1.2 What's going on? Tolerating high performance with low behaviours
Source: This figure is adapted from the work of Jack Welch.[14]

this discussion we use the terms *culture, values,* and *behaviours* loosely and interchangeably. But to clarify, an organizational culture can be examined through the values shared among members and the behaviours demonstrated by them.

Holding on to the horse's ass

'Great cultures deliver great numbers. Great numbers don't deliver great cultures. So, when you're measuring people, you've got to have a set of behaviours...like, treat people like the way you'd like to be treated yourself...You measure performance against that, against your performance in numbers'.[15] This was argued by Jack Welch during a television show in 2012. 'You put people in quadrants', he went on, and explained each of the quadrants by describing the first or top right quadrant as 'Onward and upward for these people', the second quadrant as 'Give them another chance', the third quadrant as 'Bad news. Easy. Get them out' and the top left quadrant as 'The one that kills companies – the horse's ass, the one who has cultural problems and good numbers'.[16]

But...

What is said in theory is not necessarily what is happening in practice. Even in the case of Jack Welch and General Electric. What he proclaimed isn't what GE's managers heard. 'The only things that move the culture are the ones that show up in our income statement. It's just the way we were raised', as admitted by Welch's successor Jeff Immelt in a *Harvard Business Review* interview in 2006.[17]

In other words, the horse's ass quadrant somehow got lost. The message that got through and that stuck was the overriding focus on 'making the numbers' as astutely noted by author Stephen Denning in a *Forbes*-magazine blog.[18] The message that GE managers perceived was 'good numbers *equals* onwards and upward' whereas 'bad numbers *equals* get them out'.

So, a culture of competitiveness is created where the numbers drive everything, where people compete internally, and where high performance is rewarded regardless of the display of undesired behaviours. Tolerating misbehaviours of high-performing people attributes to cultures clearly not conducive to mobilizing people for strategic organizational change. Only a healthy 'culture provides meaning, direction, and mobilization. It is the social energy that moves the corporation into allocation, the energy that flows from shared commitments among group members'.[19]

But all of this is lost when undesired behaviours from high performing people are tolerated. The social energy is lost, people are less inclined to collaborate, they retract within their own functional areas, and they withdraw extra-energies in support of wider organizational efforts. Surely holding employees accountable to be both high performers *and* demonstrate desired behaviours shouldn't be a difficult undertaking. It simply reflects the minimum behavioural and social standards required of any employee. So, it is a delusion to think that we can keep holding on to people who are 'horse's asses'.

The Customer delusion

We are all aware that customer expectations and behaviours have changed dramatically over the past decade. We are arguably in the middle of a customer revolution that is changing not only the way we produce, market, sell, and deliver our products and services today but particularly the way we need to create and deliver our customer strategies for the future.

We may well be aware but it's not necessarily reflected in our practices. Peter Drucker couldn't have put it any simpler by reminding us that 'the purpose of business is to create and keep a customer'.[20] But in how far are our strategies created from a truly customer-centric perspective? Our strategies are still too often developed in isolation of our customers or at best developed *for* them. Our customers are still too often perceived as targets and passive recipients of our products and services. Our main strategic driver is still too often to optimize and maximize our current resources and to increase sales of what we offer. We tend to be fixated on our financial growth without realizing that real growth is merely an outcome of underlying strategic offerings that are of true value to our customers.

So, we are back to a culture of the numbers: where the focus is internally driven trying to improve the bottom-line through endlessly searching for financial growth through increased performance, bigger efficiencies, higher productivity, and finding new and ingenious ways to cut costs. We are optimizing and maximizing within our own back yard and at best we are looking at creating 'customer value' from the Inside-Out. Why do we continue to do this?

Because it's much more difficult to create customer value than it is to cut cost. It's more difficult to create strategies from a customer-centric perspective than from an internal and resources-driven one. It's more difficult to come up with new value propositions than to continue milking the cash-cow.

So, a 180-degree change in mindset is required where we see, feel, think, and plan from a customer perspective first. Where we put the customer at the centre of our organizational being by placing the highest priority on the creation of enduring customer value. Where we don't create customer strategies from the Inside-Out but from the Outside-In and not in isolation but together with our customers.

It may be more difficult but it can and needs to be done. In one of his blogs, author Stephen Denning[21] puts it nicely: 'when looked at through the lens of what the firm is currently doing, value-adding opportunities will look narrow and risky. When imagination is applied from the perspective of the customer, the opportunities are boundless', even in mature markets. As examples Denning[22] refers to Amazon and Apple. By looking at the world from the customer's point of view Amazon was able to take several fully 'mature' sectors – like retail book, second-hand books, computer storage, and retail general – and turn them into high-growth businesses. Similarly, by looking at the world from the Outside-In, Apple took four slow-moving 'mature' sectors – desktop computers, music, mobile phones, and tablet computers – and turned them into explosively growing markets by adding new value to customers.

So, the critical element is to apply the imagination from the point of view of the customer first. We can't hold on to creating customer strategies from the Inside or at best from the Inside-Out. We need to adopt an Outside-In orientation. It would be a delusion to think that most of our organizations are truly customer-centric and that such orientation is embedded within our strategies, our culture, and the behaviours of every single employee. As it needs to be.

The People delusion

If we are to believe the latest Gallup's research than six out of seven employees worldwide are either 'not engaged', meaning they lack motivation and are less likely to invest discretionary effort in organizational goals, or are 'actively disengaged', indicating they are so unhappy that they will sabotage the organization.[23] Other research tells us that only 1 in 10 employees are truly mobilsed.[24] With 'mobilized' we mean people who can, know, and want to exert extra-energies to help realize organizational change on top of their day-to-day operational challenges.

It's hard to believe such shocking results. Then again our own empirical research into organizational disengagement indicates similar findings.[25] But whether it's only 1 out of 7 employees who is highly engaged or 2 or 3 out of 7, the fact is that we are failing to gain a critical mass of people who want to exert extra-energies for the betterment of the wider organization.

Here are some additional appalling statistics from a recent Deloitte study[26] of 2,500 organizations in 90 countries which found that 86 per cent of business leaders don't believe they have an adequate leadership pipeline; 75 per cent are struggling to attract and recruit the top people they need; only 6 per cent believe their current process for managing performance is worth the time; and only 17 per cent feel that they have a compelling employment brand.

What's going on? What kinds of environments have been created within our organizations for such inexcusable statistics to be the outcomes? Alarmingly, the distressing engagement statistics are only part of the problem.

First of all we tend to make little distinction between organization and job engagement. Most concepts focus mainly on engagement with the job. What this means in our context is that if people aren't even engaged within their jobs then it's very unlikely for them to be engaged with the wider organization and would want to realize any organizational strategic change.

Secondly, engagement, whilst critical, 'only' relates to the *Want*. People may be engaged at both job and organizational level and wanting to support organizational change but they may not *Know* or understand the required change or how to contribute. In other words, they aren't strategically aligned and leadership has failed to contextualize the organizational strategy and make it meaningful across all levels of the organization.

Finally, the most basic level relates to the *Can*. But a large shortfall of workforce capability has been identified as a top urgent global trend. Within our organizations we struggle to have the right number of people in the right jobs at the right level at the right time with the right competencies and the right skills. It would be a delusion to think that today's capability gap is limited to engineers and scientists. In addition to the need for technical skills organizations are also facing shortages especially in first-line supervisors throughout sales, customer service, manufacturing, finance, and other business functions.[27] This gap is of significant strategic importance. Because again it would be a delusion to think that any organizational strategic change can be realized without a critical mass of especially supervisors and middle managers who Can, let alone Know and Want.

The overwhelmed employee

How do we expect to gain a critical mass of people who want to realize organizational strategic change when two out of three of today's employees feel 'overwhelmed' in their day-to-day jobs?[28] How do people deal with the flood of information, the text messages, tweets, the 200-plus emails on average, the checking of the mobile phone 150 times on average, the meetings, and conference calls *every day*?[29] The simple answer is they don't.

The Deloitte research tells us that people are working too hard and that the concept of work–life balance has become a delusion thanks to the proliferation of technology and the breakdown in barriers between work and life.[30] Reference is made to research by neurologist Larry Rosen, who reveals that the average office worker can focus only for seven minutes at a time before they either switch windows or check Facebook.[31] So, it shouldn't be surprising that all of this causes distraction, stress, and general reduction in productivity as reiterated by blogger Josh Bersin.[32] Altogether not exactly the ideal environment to realizing any organizational strategic change effort.

The unrecognized employee

Our research found that the single most important and generic driver for employees to exert extra-energies and help realize organizational change is recognition.[33] But incredibly the majority of people in our organizations don't feel recognized for their contributions. We feel that the concept of recognition isn't well understood and is often confused with reward.

Many people-managers come up with delusional excuses for not recognizing their staff such as[34] 'I don't have the time to recognise everyone differently' or 'My team is too large' or 'I'll never remember when the time comes' or most distressingly 'I don't want to know because then I will be expected to do it'. So, perplexingly there are not many managers out there who recognize their staff sincerely, informally, personally, timely, and specifically.

What's going on? Again, how can we expect for people to go into-fifth-gear and support organizational change on top of being overwhelmed within their day-to-day operational jobs and without them feeling valued, understood, and recognized?

The Leadership delusion

So, let's dare to ask ourselves a direct question: 'Who is ultimately responsible for today's strategy delusions in relation to Change, Planning, Customers, People, and Behaviours?' The answer leads to the ultimate delusion regarding our beliefs about 'leadership'. Let's explore further.

When you type in the word *leadership* in Amazon's book section you get more than a 100,000 books that have been written on the topic. Yes, more than a 100,000 books. 'There are almost as many different definitions of leadership as there are persons who have attempted to define the concept' as noted more than four decades ago by Stogdill.[35]

There are dozens of academic leadership philosophies or concepts as illustrated in Figure 1.3. The result of all of this is that no single leadership definition or concept exists that satisfies all commentators.

Appreciative leadership Transformational leadership Contextual leadership Servant leadership Contingency leadership Emotional leadership Charismatic leadership Empowerment leadership Ethical leadership Functional leadership Authentic leadership Implicit leadership Managerial leadership Relational leadership Situational leadership Behavioural leadership Spiritual leadership Sustainability leadership Participatory leadership Trait leadership Meta leadership Transactional leadership Vales-based leadership Action-centred leadership Engaged leadership Mindful leadership Integrated leadership Adaptive leadership

---

Figure 1.3 What's going on? A selection of 'leadership' philosophies and concepts

How can we argue against, for example, being an appreciative, authentic, ethical, mindful, transformational, and values-based leader? Obviously we can't. But what we seem to have forgotten in all of this – both in theory and in practice – is that leadership ultimately is about *direction*. Manfred de Vries reminds us that the Anglo–Saxon etymological root of the words 'lead, leader, and leadership' is *laed* which means path or road.[36] So, the second we call ourselves a 'leader' surely we are consumed with realizing our organizational path or road or preferred direction?

We provocatively and frankly would argue: NO! Based on our own research and observations we see the majority of leaders in today's organizations being overwhelmed with *managing* day-to-day operational challenges. Our leaders seem besieged, snowed-under, inundated, and paralysed with trying to manage the daily demands and complications of organizational life today. So, longer-term strategic leadership has lost out to short-term operational management.

Getting rid of the rhetoric

When you get rid of all the drama and all the rhetoric, when you distil all the hoopla down to nuts and bolts, what is leadership all about? It is about realizing some kind of direction, intent, or vision through people. Realizing a preferred direction or vision means automatically realizing some sort of strategic change. But this often seems to get lost in all of today's leadership rhetoric.

If we can't get strategic change done, our leadership is at best questionable. 'You can stand on a mountaintop and preach. You can paint the most beautiful visions of the future. If nothing gets done, does it really matter? Leadership is not simply about vision; it's about your capacity to be proactive and your ability to translate your vision into real results. Leadership is not simply about inspiration; it's about your capacity to translate your vision into a concrete agenda. Leadership is not simply about charisma. Leadership is about getting people on your side, sustaining momentum, and keeping them on your side'.[37]

So, in this book we directly link leadership to strategic change as well as to a social practice. A social practice because people are the ultimate enabling factor to making any strategic change happening. We subsequently define *leadership* as:

Enabling and mobilizing people who Can, Know, and Want to create and realize a preferred direction.

In terms of the *strategic* aspect of leadership – as discussed earlier – we see many of today's leaders either holding on or being overwhelmed with managing day-to-day operational complexities often at the expense of realizing distinctive strategies. In terms of the *social* aspect of leadership we also observe many organizational leaders failing to gain a critical mass of people who Can, Know, and Want to realize strategic change on top of their day-to-day challenges. We believe that it has become the ultimate strategic leadership challenge in organizational life today.

In search of the right leaders

If the ability to mobilize people is such a critical leadership challenge then the question becomes, "do we have the right leaders with the right qualities to achieve this?" When exploring this question within academic and practice literatures more than a hundred typically desired leadership traits and attributes can be identified as illustrated in Figure 1.4.

Honest Communicator Listener Confident Committed Energetic Authentic Delegator Inspiring Positive Ethical Giving recognition Intuitive Values-driven Visionary Emotionally Intelligent Integrity Sets priorities Motivator Entrepreneurial Compassionate Action-orientated Focussed Open to change Respectful Caring Clear Decisive Empathetic Collaborative Humble Mindful Self-aware Supportive Engaging Wise Passionate Open minded Creative Results-driven Social Pro-active Unselfish Facilitating Giving feedback Flexible Resourceful Approachable Rewarding Consistent Evaluative Initiator Optimistic Self-controlling Courageous Responsible Understanding Good sense of judgement Strategic Effective Original Humorous Alert Insightful Persistent Conscientious Role-model Trustworthy Assertive Adaptable Problem-solver Imaginative Fair Straightforward Loyal Tactful Candid Appreciative Enabler Walks-the-talk Dedicated Culturally aware Cooperative Intelligent Risk-taker Extrovert Accountable Change-master Team builder Story-teller Ambitious Realistic Learner Strong work-ethic Imaginative Of good character Accessible Determined Influencer Customer-focused Relationship building Transparent Stable Creative Decision-taker Commercially driven Inclusive

Figure 1.4 What's going on? A 100-plus typically desired leadership traits and attributes

An observation is that the desired leadership traits and attributes as illustrated in Figure 1.3 seem to relate to the more behavioural aspects of leadership. They all appear *people* related as opposed to specific competencies, skills, or expertise. Many leaders may be experts in some functional field but what is their track-record in gaining critical mass amongst their people who Can, Know, and Want to help realize strategic change?

Surely we can't expect a leader to possess all or most of the identified traits and attributes as depicted in Figure 1.3. But recent global research by Deloitte points to seven *foundational* ones urgently required in today's market environment as illustrated in Figure 1.5

---

1. Customer-centricity

Enhancing effective customer relationships

2. Creativity

Driving innovation and entrepreneurship

3. Influence & inspiration

Setting direction and driving employees to achieve business goals

4. Building teams & talent

Developing people and creating effective teams

5. Collaboration

Having the ability to build cross-functional teams

6. Business acumen

Understanding the core business well

7. Cultural agility

Managing diversity and inclusion

Figure 1.5 In need of twenty-first-century leadership: seven foundational traits and attributes[38]

So, the search is on for leaders at all levels who – at least – are customer-centric, creative, inspirational, team-builders, collaborators, commercially aware, and culturally agile. Clearly twentieth-century leadership practices such as command-and-control do nothing to mobilize people for change enduringly. And we can't forget that power is ultimately given to leaders. Being a leader doesn't automatically mean we deserve to be a leader or we have a right to lead others. The privilege to lead others is always granted. In other words being a leader means that some of us have been placed in a prominent position to *serve* others: to serve our customers, our communities, our boards, our investors, and arguably most importantly our people.[39] This 'serving' aspect of leadership can't be forgotten.

The 'strategic delusions' in relation to Change, Planning, Customer, People, Behaviour, and Leadership as highlighted in this opening chapter may well explain the high failure rates when it comes to making strategy happen. They also may explain the dramatic shortening of life expectancy for many of our organizations. Among *Fortune* 500 companies the life expectancy has fallen from 75 years half a century ago to only 15 years today and quickly heading towards 10 to 5 years unless there is change.[40]

We simply can't accept ingrained business models, periodic and monopolized planning, internally driven strategies, overwhelmed and unrecognized employees, twentieth-century leadership styles, and cultures that accept high performance at the detriment of desired behaviours.

We can't keep holding on to the nut as per our earlier monkey-trap example. We need to let go and see, feel, think, plan, and act…differently. This is explored in the following chapters of this book!

2
Strategic Sensing – Not Just Thinking

Imagine you are visiting Chicago for the first time. You head straight to the Skydeck on the 103rd floor of the Willis Tower, the tallest skyscraper in the city. At the Skydeck, you ask four people at random to have a look and share their definition of Chicago with you. The first person may look to the *north* and define Chicago as being affluent pointing out the beautiful suburbs and parks. The second person may look *east*, to the famous shores of Lake Michigan and describe Chicago as being all about recreation, sailing and playing volleyball on the beaches. The third person may peer to the *south* and define Chicago as being poor and dangerous pointing out the ghettos and gangs. And, the fourth person may look to the *west* and define Chicago as being industrial describing the numerous factories and plants.

What happened in this analogy is symbolic for what often happens in organizational life. Whenever we are exposed to something new, we tend to rationalize it through our own lens or, to stick with our analogy, a 'north view' paradigm. We try and make sense of the new situation based on our own 'limited' experiences and preconceived beliefs. Many individual employees examine situations from their respective 'north views' often based on their own functional expertise and specific experiences. This phenomenon can also apply to groups of people united by common beliefs or purpose. Whole departments, divisions and organizations tend to develop strategies from within their collective 'north views'. But meaningful strategies cannot be developed within a 'north view' paradigm only. It requires managers to step out of their 'north views'. Managers who, for instance, on the

Willis Tower can build a 360-degree picture and define Chicago as being affluent and beautiful in the north, all about sport and recreation in the east, as being poor and dangerous in the south, and industrial in the west. Through the Willis Tower analogy, we highlight the importance of breaking through traditionally held 'north views' as it severely limits our strategic thinking.

Trapped in the north view

It is impossible to develop strategies without engaging in strategic thinking. The problem is that many executives and managers struggle with thinking strategically. We often hear executives complain about the strategic thinking capabilities of their managers.[1] At the same time, the lack of strategic thinking amongst executives themselves has been identified in various studies.[2]

Why does this 'strategic thinking gap' exist within most organizations? One explanation relates to many leaders and managers wrongly assuming that strategic planning, strategic development and strategic thinking are all synonymous.[3] There is an important distinction. Strategic thinking should produce insights, which become inputs to the strategic development and planning processes. That is why no strategies can be developed, let alone planned for, without engaging in strategic thinking. Another explanation relates to many of us finding it difficult to shift our thinking from a shorter term and operational focus to a longer term strategic one. It is not without reason that Henry Mintzberg regards strategic thinking as 'an immensely complex process, which involves the most sophisticated, subtle, and at times subconscious elements of human thinking'.[4]

The strategic thinking gap can leave us in a vulnerable position, especially in today's fast changing and competitive environment. Change is constant but what is less obvious is that today's change is often non-linear. Linear change involves cause-and-effect or sequential occurrences while non-linear change is often characterised by surprise and uncertainty. Most of our strategic development is still rooted in linear cause-and-effect thinking. There is a complexity about today's dynamic environment, which defies linear and accustomed ways of thinking. Traditional thinking and reactive acting can leave organizations exposed. Customer needs must be anticipated before they are perceived and problems must be anticipated before they manifest themselves. Strategic thought that mainly seeks hard, fact-based and logical information may have been sufficient in more stable or slower changing environments. But 'the dogmas of the quiet past are inadequate to the stormy present...as our case is new, so we must think anew and act anew', as Abraham Lincoln said. We believe that organizations now require distinctive strategies that originate in insights beyond the reach of conventional thinking. Good insights help us uncover opportunities for creating customer value and points of distinction. They help us understand the fundamental drivers of our business and challenge assumptions about our existing value propositions.

Coming back to our analogy, how can we think of distinctive strategies if we keep developing them from a 'north view'? Surely, discovering insights requires a 'global view' that deals with each case and situation with all of their dimensions in an unusual way. It is a rare and urgently needed capability, which lies at the core of developing strategic change but is not widely practiced. The fact that so many organizations remain 'trapped in their north view' may explain why 'we have today a massive epidemic of institutional failure'. Dee Hoch, founder and ex-chairman of Visa and ex-CEO of the Bank of America, said:[5]

> You can look around you: schools that can't teach, welfare systems in which nobody fares well, unhealthy healthcare systems, corporations that can't compete, economies that can't economise, police that can't enforce the law, judicial systems without justice.

The list is virtually endless of organizations increasingly unable to achieve the purpose for which they profess to exist. Let alone being able to develop distinctive strategies and deliver enduring value.

In search of D-options

Let us assume you own a two-seater sports car and you live and work in London. It is a cold winter's day and whilst driving home from work you notice three people waiting at a bus stop in this miserable weather. The first person waiting is A) an old lady who looks like she is about to die. The second person is B) an old mate who once saved your life. The third person C) seems to be the partner of your dreams. You have only a two-seater sports car so what do you do?

We sometimes ask our audiences this exact question. Typically, the audience will respond in a predictable fashion where roughly one-third will put their hands up and choose the old lady, one-third will choose their best mate, and the rest of the audience will go for their perceived dream partner. Whatever the selection is, we probably can come up with a rational argument for each of the alternatives. In a way, this is not dissimilar as how we tend to develop strategies; we look for typical A, B or C options. It is very rare for somebody in the audience to come up with a D-option in which, for instance, you give the keys of your sports car to your best mate and ask him to take the old lady to the hospital so that you can wait with the partner of your dreams for the next bus.

Our argument is that in today's uncertain environment there is an urgent need for D-options. For example, the pursuit of cost-cutting and downsizing in today's economic climate is typically seen as a rational strategy and as cloned and learned responses to uncertainty. It is difficult to argue against becoming 'lean and mean'. Even though in some cases the rationality could be debated of 'knee-jerk' cuttings associated with what we call 'corporate anorexia'. The point is that whilst we are busy carrying out cost-cutting strategies we are giving ourselves a false sense of security. We may have come up with 'rational' A, B, or C strategies as per our earlier analogy. But such strategies merely deal with the internal effects and are not addressing the underlying external challenges facing the business. Or, as Steve Jobs at Apple stated: 'A lot of companies have chosen to downsize, and maybe that was the right thing for them. We chose a different path. Our belief was that if we kept putting great products in front of customers, they would continue to open their wallets'.[6] Having the external and creative insight to come up with D-options like the iPhone or iPad product offerings is of course much harder. It is easier to merely being consumed with internal downsizing strategies. However, D-options are needed addressing novel and creative ways of demonstrating value to our customers. There is an urgent need to see, feel and think differently to enable the discovery of such convention-breaking insights.

What do we mean by 'insights'? As some scholars eloquently explain: 'An insight is a sudden and unexpected solution to a problem. Arrived at after an impasse has been reached and an incubation period has elapsed. The point at which the solution occurs is sometimes referred to as an 'eureka' moment ... An incubation period is often necessary for insight to occur because it enables non-conscious processes to operate more freely by relaxing constraints imposed by rational analysis'.[7] For insights to be discovered, the role of rationale and reason ought to be played down in favour of more non-conscious and non-rational practices. Or perhaps as Einstein said, 'Logic will get you from A to B. Imagination will get you everywhere'.[8] Many of today's organizations are in need of imaginative D-options that originate in eureka moments beyond the reach of conventional rational thinking. This can only achieved only through what we call 'strategic sensing'.

The need for strategic sensing

Distinctive strategies can be unlocked through *strategic sensing*, which we define as a process of discovering insights through seeing, feeling and thinking strategically. In order to think strategically, we also need to be able to see and feel strategically.

Three states of strategic sensing are illustrated in our Sensing Model for Seeing, Feeling and Thinking Strategically (see Figure 2.1). In the *Inside Sensing* state, we tend to develop strategies within our own paradigm based on linear and analytical thought. In this rational state, sensing through feeling or intuition is not really valued. This state is mostly internally driven and strategic seeing is limited to our 'north view'. In the *Inside-Out Sensing* state, we try to, some extent, analyse the external environment but remain driven and influenced by our own paradigm. We look at the external environment from a 'north view' perspective and particularly select data that 'proves' our own hypotheses. In this state, not a lot of strategic intuition is applied and strategies are mainly based on rational and linear thought. Truly distinctive strategies, however, are developed in the *Outside-In Sensing* state where the starting point for all our sensing is always externally driven. We start from customer, market and stakeholder perspectives first, not our own internally resources or capabilities perspectives. In this state, we sense more like entrepreneurs and identify, often through non-linear thinking, opportunities where others do not. We attempt to exploit those opportunities without regard to resources currently controlled.

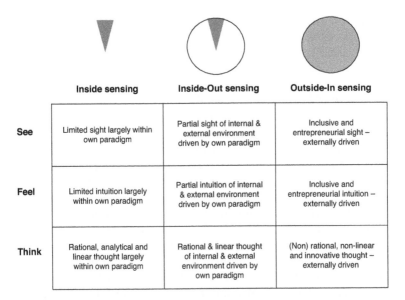

	Inside sensing	Inside-Out sensing	Outside-In sensing
See	Limited sight largely within own paradigm	Partial sight of internal & external environment driven by own paradigm	Inclusive and entrepreneurial sight – externally driven
Feel	Limited intuition largely within own paradigm	Partial intuition of internal & external environment driven by own paradigm	Inclusive and entrepreneurial intuition – externally driven
Think	Rational, analytical and linear thought largely within own paradigm	Rational & linear thought of internal & external environment driven by own paradigm	(Non) rational, non-linear and innovative thought – externally driven

Figure 2.1 Sensing model for seeing, feeling and thinking strategically

Distinctive strategies cannot be thought of without stretching strategic seeing and feeling as illustrated in our model. Stretching our seeing and feeling, and therefore our thinking, from the Outside-In is easier said than done.

Stretching seeing

The problem is that we are often unaware that we develop strategies from a 'north view'. The unconsciousness in which we see only what we select to see and then act on those observations can have grave consequences. Such unawareness can lead to 'skilled incompetence' where we develop and implement ineffective strategies with great skill but without recognizing that we are merely 'puzzling solving' within our own paradigm. We typically attribute the undesired outcomes to anyone or anything but ourselves. Most of the time, 'unforeseeable' variables are blamed for not realizing our strategic objectives like the external markets, the global economy or increasing competition. The difficultly with this unconsciousness is that we remain unable to change recurrent patterns behind our failure to see and therefore think differently. We find ourselves in a causal loop of inference but our inferences may be totally wrong and the strategic plans we develop and act upon unwarranted.

If we believe it then we will see it

A popular proverb says 'seeing is believing' but as the philosopher George Santayana[9] pointed out, humans are much better at believing than at seeing. We tend to see mainly what we believe and then act on those beliefs. An explanation as to why this happens relates to the Ladder of Inference as developed by organizational psychologist Chris Argyris[10] and used by Peter Senge in his popular book *The Fifth Discipline*[11]. By linking The Ladder of Inference to strategy development, it is helpful in guiding our understanding of how we make inferences based on self-generating beliefs, which limit our seeing, our thinking and ultimately our creation of distinct strategies. Our ability to achieve strategic change is eroded from the start by assuming that our beliefs are the truth, the truth is obvious, our beliefs are based on real data, and the data we select are the real data.

In the context of strategy development, the Ladder of Inference in Figure 2.2 explains how our beliefs affect what data we select to 'see'. In any situation there is an infinite pool of available data that we can tune into. However, none of us do. It is difficult because we are exposed to such large amounts of data. For instance, external data related to political, economical, social, technological, environmental, regulatory, market, customer, and competitor variables in addition to internal organizational data. So, what we do is *filter* and *select* data in order to simplify and manage the information. We pay no or little attention to the rest of the data. This phenomenon is coined 'anti-library' by Nassim Nicholas Taleb[12] in his book *The Black Swan* where he argues that the unread books in one's personal library are far more important than the read books. Taleb's anti-library concept embodies the limitations of a 'north view' or the idea that what we don't know is probably more important than what we do know. From the selected data, we then step up the ladder and add subjective *meaning* to our selected data. We create a story, a theory or interpretation about what is happening based on the data we selected to see. Once we have selected certain data and given it meaning then very quickly we step

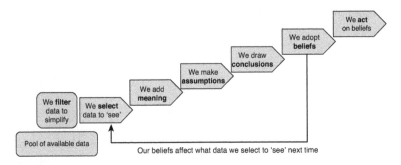

Figure 2.2 Using the Ladder of Inference in understanding limited or partial strategic sight

Source: Adapted from the work of Chris Argyris (1990) and Peter Senge (1994).

up the ladder and make *assumptions* about our external and internal environment. At this stage we construct hypotheses from the inferences we made and determine what our strategic alternatives are. Then we start to draw *conclusions* and make decisions about what our strategic objectives are in accordance with our earlier constructed hypotheses. It is then a small step to firming up or *adopting* a belief. Or as philosopher Robert Anton Wilson[13] said 'we believe what we see and then we believe our interpretation of it, we don't even know we are making an interpretation most of the time. We think this is reality'. So, we have created a 'plausible' interpretation of reality and then take *action* based on our beliefs. Ironically, our beliefs then affect what data we select to 'see' next time. The data ignored will often disconfirm our beliefs if we paid any attention to it. We find ourselves in a self-reinforcing loop of inference based on a 'north view' resulting in an inability to see differently, develop distinctive strategies and realize strategic change.

How to see differently?

The first corrective step is to be conscious of our natural tendency to climb that ladder of inference which limits us to seeing a 'north view' only. We need to be conscious of being 'trapped in a north view' and invite different paradigms within our strategic development practices. This inevitably means that many of our assumptions and beliefs that we take for granted as being self-evidently true may have to be abandoned. 'You can't solve the problem with the same reasoning that caused the problem', as Einstein famously said. The task of changing beliefs within any organization is not to be underestimated. It probably is the biggest challenge to seeing strategically. When our ingrained beliefs are challenged, we build up fences around us to maintain our ideological defences. The paradox is that we all can see how other people's beliefs make them 'blind' at times but we find it very hard to be conscious how our own beliefs are doing the same to us.

The second corrective step is to step outside our 'north view' and start seeing from the Outside-In looking for data from an external perspective first. It is about what management author Fred Kofman calls the need for an 'empathy shift' where you abandon the logic of your own perspective and are able to see (and feel) from others' perspectives. He goes on to say that it is about losing your self-righteousness and becoming curious about the data that supports other perspectives.[14]

Another related step is to be conscious of different ways of seeing the 'same'. We all have our own 'reality tunnel' according to psychologist Timothy Leary.[15] With a subconscious set of mental filters formed from our individual beliefs and experiences, every individual interprets the same world differently hence 'Truth is in the eye of the beholder'. Returning to our 'north view' analogy, even though a person may have the capability of seeing a 360-degree picture and define Chicago from the four cardinal views, when it comes to the actual description, for instance, of the south being 'poor and dangerous', who says that is a correct or true account? Imagine if same question was asked to a person from Yemen. He or she may disagree with the south side of Chicago being 'poor and dangerous' and argue: 'Everybody wears Nike trainers and owns a colour television. Okay, some kids carry pistols but back in Yemen we've got 60 million weapons for a population of 20 million, which means each person owns three weapons on average and not 'just' pistols but Kalashnikovs, rocket-propelled grenades and bazookas. Now that's a dangerous place'. In other words, there are different ways of looking at exactly the 'same' or 'a different point of view is simply the view from a place where you're not'.

This principle and slogan was cleverly used by HSBC in an advertisement campaign in which the Bank used antonyms to describe the same object (Figure 2.3).

Figure 2.3   A different point of view
Source: Photographer: Henrik Knudsen. Printed with permission from HSBC Holdings plc.

What the HSBC campaign does is challenge our own 'north view' or reality. It highlights that any given perspective is simply one way of seeing things. When our 'north view' is compared with others, responses are often varied and may be so different that they are complete opposites. The point we are making is that the 'north view' analogy, the Ladder of Inference, the Reality Tunnel theory, and the HSBC campaign concept are all applicable to any organization or department attempting to develop strategies. Distinctive strategies cannot be thought of when they are developed within a 'north view' paradigm, when other perspectives of the 'north view' itself are not sought, and when the 'east, south and west views' are not, or partly, identified and evaluated.

Stretching feeling

First of all, what do we mean by *feeling*? Feeling in the context of our sensing model is the use of intuition or 'gut feeling'. To be able to think of strategic insights, we need to stretch our seeing but also our feeling as described in our Sensing model. Strategic feeling ought to be an incredibly important capability for organizational leaders and managers.

Why strategic intuition?

Why is strategic feeling as a sensing capability becoming so important? We believe that conventional strategic thinking on its own will not provide the 'answers'. In our search for convention-breaking insights we will have no choice but to increase our non-conscious sensing and free ourselves from the intrusion of rational thought and logical inference. With increasing complexity and uncertainty in most business environments, we simply don't have the points of reference related to the new complex conditions that we are or will be facing. Not surprisingly, the conditions where intuition functions best, according to scholars,[16] are: when a high level of uncertainty exists, when little previous precedent exists, when variables are less rationally predictable, when facts are limited or do not clearly point the way to go, when analytical data is of limited use; when several plausible alternative solutions exist to choose from with good arguments for each and when time is limited and there is pressure to come up with the right strategic decision.

Managers-as-entrepreneurs learning from entrepreneurs-as-managers

Given that most of us are managing under the previously described conditions, we can expect having to rely increasingly on intuition as part of our strategic sensing. From an organizational perspective there is arguably an increasing need for 'managers as entrepreneurs'. Empirical research[17] tells us that entrepreneurs are more able to live with or even thrive on conditions of ambiguity and uncertainty. It is because of entrepreneurial traits like self-sufficiency and self-efficacy where entrepreneurs tend to trust their own judgement. Entrepreneurs are also willing to take decisions even though they may not have all the information they need at hand. When outcomes are difficult to predict through rational means and strategic decisions need to be made, they respond in a pragmatic way by utilizing their intuition to take such decisions. They dare to take an intuitive stand and leave out 'paralysis by analysis'. Academics agree that the nature of entrepreneurship and the style of entrepreneurs is, by necessity, more intuitive than rational.[18] This is confirmed by Richard Branson who claims: 'I never get the accountants in before I start a business. It's done on gut feeling'.[19] Other successful entrepreneurs like Bill Gates, Oprah Winfrey and Steve Jobs attribute their success to their intuition[20] and having the courage to follow their hearts. So, can we learn from successful 'entrepreneurs as managers'?

Emulating entrepreneurial sensing

In the context of strategic sensing what is it about entrepreneurs and being entrepreneurial that we can learn from? Broadly speaking, entrepreneurs innovate whereas many of us imitate. Conceptually the distinction is clear. Where the entrepreneur is the pioneer, the manager is the applier of existing best practice. Where the entrepreneur engages in strategic activity, the manager focuses on tactical or operational activity. The irrefutable difference between entrepreneurs and most of us in institutional life is their openness to sense and exploit opportunities everywhere and at anytime. They start sensing from an external perspective and without regard to resources currently controlled. Entrepreneurs have an innate ability to sense for opportunities through seeing, feeling and thinking differently from the Outside-In.

What do we mean by everywhere and anytime in a practical sense? *Everywhere* means being in a position to sense across all customer touch-points exploring what can be done, for instance, better, quicker, cheaper, differently, faster, more conveniently, more reliably, safer or more consistently. *Anytime* means seeing, feeling and thinking of such opportunities on a continuing basis instead of once a year during a strategic planning session.

Because entrepreneurs sense opportunities from the Outside-In they don't feel constrained by potential lack of resources or capabilities like most of us do in institutional life. Entrepreneurs sense options beyond today's reality and they don't let the current state of affairs have too much impact on their future decisions. They start by sensing how to generate value from a true market and customer perspective first. Once customer value has been identified this is turned into the 'size-of-the-prize' which then justifies overcoming internal disenabling factors. In contrast, many of us in institutional life start from the Inside-Out. We therefore don't see the true external potential because we are too quick in dismissing it due to 'limited' available resources. Many of us tend to analyse and think of the many reasons why a new initiative cannot succeed. Entrepreneurs dare to sense differently, speedily and big. Sensing the bigger picture, or holism, was found to be the most important element of intuitive decision-making among entrepreneurs in empirical research on entrepreneurial intuition.[21]

What exactly is strategic intuition?

It is an indispensable component of strategic sensing. Intuition should not be confused with instinct. Instinct is more like a reflex action such as a 'knee-jerk' reaction. It is a quick and impulsive action. In our view, intuition is much more. A good description from a strategy perspective is described in a *Long Range Planning* article titled 'Intuition in Organizations: Implications for Strategic Management'. According to the authors, intuition comprises of the following:[22]

1. A capacity for attaining direct knowledge or understanding without the apparent intrusion of rational thought or logical inference
2. Neither the opposite of rationality, nor a random process of guessing, intuition corresponds to thoughts, conclusions and choices produced largely or in part through non-conscious mental processes
3. Affectively charged judgements that arise through rapid, non-conscious and holistic associations

It is important to clarify that intuition is not the same as insight. As the authors of the earlier article explain intuition may presage insight. Or, intuitions are intimations of insights experienced as feeling of knowing.

We believe there are three different types of intuition related to strategic sensing. They are Opportunity intuition, Action intuition and Social intuition. *Opportunity intuition* relates to *feeling what* the future direction needs to be from the Outside-In. It relates to the openness and ability to discover opportunities resulting from non-conscious and holistic sensing. Entrepreneurial managers possessing opportunistic intuition are able to *feel beyond* as opposed to merely *see ahead*. The latter foresees an expected future by constructing a framework out of the events of the past. The former, sensing beyond, constructs the future itself and a world that would not otherwise be.[23] Opportunity intuition is arguably described in one of Steve Jobs' famous quotes:[24]

> You can't connect the dots looking forward; you can only connect them looking backwards. So you have to trust that the dots will somehow connect in your future. You have to trust in something: your gut, destiny, life, karma, whatever. Because believing that the dots will connect down the road will give you the confidence to follow your heart, even when it leads you off the well worn path.

Action intuition relates to *feeling how* the future desired-state needs to be realized from the Outside-In. It is the ability to feel how best the vision can be realized through the creation of customer-centric objectives. We link the ability to not only understand but also feel like a customer – or customer empathy – directly to Action intuition. Managers possessing Action intuition know what it feels like to 'walk-in-their-customer's-shoes' and sense innovative ways of creating value together with their customers. They realize that only customer-centric strategies can be turned into enduring execution. And, they focus on overcoming internal factors that can disenable implementation.

The ability to non-conventionally feel what and how the vision should be implemented is a very special ability. But it all is a bit of a theoretical exercise if we then actually fail to build a critical mass of People who will support the implementation of the developed vision and strategic objectives. Our workforce is the ultimate enabling factor in making any strategic change happen. Managers who possess *Social intuition* not only understand this but also have the ability to *feel who* amongst their workforce are or are not supporting the strategic change. They feel what the important drivers are from a true People's perspective. Such People centricity helps them in mobilizing a critical mass of the workforce willing to go the extra-mile and exert extra-energies to making strategic change happen, on top of their day-to-day operational challenges.

Not Prozac intuition

Often intuitive entrepreneurs and their positive leadership practices are seen as glorying in an exposure to risk. They are referred to as Prozac leaders by David Collinson from Lancaster University. They discourage critical thinking in favour of high and intuitive risk taking. Prozac leaders not only are over-optimistic themselves, but they also demand constant positivity in their followers. 'They often refuse to heed cautionary voices and alternative views, effectively silencing criticism, which can lead to a culture of excessive risk taking'.[25] The ramifications of Prozac leadership and Prozac intuition can be disastrous. In his article, Collinsson refers to the former President of Lehman Brothers Joe Gregory, who prided himself on making decisions based on intuition rather than detailed risk analysis.

Clearly Prozac intuition is not what we are advocating in this chapter. It is true that entrepreneurial managers are less risk averse than the average manager. However, enduring entrepreneurial practices do require risk control. This is an important facet of any entrepreneurial strategic seeing, feeling and thinking. The goal of entrepreneurial managers is to make above-normal profits but at risk levels typically no higher than the norm in their industry.[26]

So, we are not advocating that 'reason is, and only ought be, the slave of the passions' as once proclaimed by David Hume, the famous Scottish philosopher.[27] What we have argued is that many of today's organizations are in need of imaginative D-options that originate in eureka moments beyond the reach of conventional thinking. This is achieved only through creating and acting on distinctive strategies that are unlocked through *strategic sensing*, which we defined as a process of discovering insights through seeing, feeling *and* thinking strategically as explored in this chapter.

Collective continuous sensing

Seeing, feeling and thinking from the Outside-In can be done individually but should be practiced collaboratively. The diffusion of strategic sensing capabilities throughout the organization typically presents a big challenge. Strategic sensing is a critical capability that should take place at multiple levels across the organization and not be limited to the top echelons. Collective strategic sensing creates better insights. It enables a proactive and creative dialogue where we gain each other's perspectives and where we can rigorously and playfully challenge conventional thinking about the fundamental drivers for our markets, customers and people. It won't just happen nor can it be done in a few scheduled strategic planning meetings. It is a cultural and behavioural practice that should be on-going instead of episodic. Strategic sensing never stops.

3
Co-Creating a Compelling Story

Strategic change efforts fail when they are internally driven and developed within our own paradigm based on conventional thinking as discussed in the previous chapter. Another critical reason why many strategies fail is the inability of leaders to mobilize their workforce and realize the proposed strategic change. In other words, failing to get a critical mass of people who Can, Know and/or Want to make strategic change happen on top of their day-to-day operational challenges. We believe it is the ultimate challenge to realizing enduring strategic change within most organizations.

The mobilizing challenge: people who Can, Know and Want

At the most basic level, we obviously need to ensure that people actually *can* and are proficient to fulfil the strategic change requirements. Does the majority of the workforce possess the right competencies and skills to implement the developed strategic change requirements? These required skills may well differ from current day-to-day operational ones. The second criteria in addition to being proficient relates to the *know* or in how far people are strategically aligned with proposed change. Does a critical mass of our people cognitively understand the change requirements for the organization? And, have we been able to contextualize and make it meaningful across the various levels of the organization?

Securing a critical mass of people who Can and Know is in itself not an easy task. But the fundamental question then becomes: Have we ensured a critical mass of people who are not only proficient and

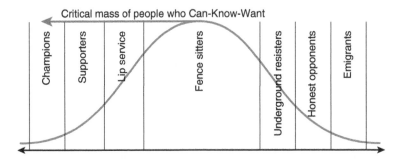

Figure 3.1 Mobilizing a critical mass of people who Can-Know-Want

strategically aligned but who also are strategically engaged and *want* to exert extra-energies for the betterment of the wider organization?

Getting a critical mass of people within any organization who Can-Know-Want is a challenge. We illustrate this in Figure 3.1 albeit in an oversimplified yet practical manner. When trying to mobilize people and realize strategic change, a workforce generally resembles the standard deviation as depicted in Figure 3.1. They tend to be divided across the following 'typologies'.

Starting on the left of Figure 3.1 are the *Champions*. They represent a small section of the workforce but are keen to champion or lead the strategic change. They are proficient, strategically aligned and willing to exert extra-energies to leading proposed change happen. The next and slightly larger group are the *Supporters*. They won't actually lead but are willing to at least support the implementation of developed strategic change. Moving on to the right of Figure 3.1 is group who typically pay *Lip Service* to the proposed change. No matter what kind of strategic change is being initiated they will pay lip service and on the whole go along with it. But the largest group within the standard deviation of a typical organization are the *Fence Sitters*. The members of this significant group tend to be quite apathetic to change. They are uninterested, indifferent and unresponsive to being involved in making the strategic change happen. Moving to the right of the standard deviation are the *Underground Resisters*. This group of the workforce is not only opposed to the proposed change but covertly resist it. They try and undermine any progress in a stealthily fashion. This group is sometimes symbolically and blatantly compared with 'putting one rotten apple in a drum of apples...it impacts the healthy apples around it'. Then we move down the right of the standard deviation to the *Honest Opponents*. This group also oppose the proposed strategic change but they actively and openly challenge it. This is an important group in any organization and not to be dismissed. The fact that members of this group openly and honestly oppose the change often means that they are engaged and do care. They may well represent a 'south view' referring back to the analogy used in our previous chapter. Lastly and on the far right of the standard deviation are the *Emigrants* and they... emotionally have left the building, so to speak.

At the end of the day making strategic change happen is truly a people's game. People are the ultimate enabling factor in moving from strategic plans to enduring execution. We may have succeeded in developing distinctive strategies through seeing, feeling and thinking differently. But it all is a bit of a theoretical exercise if the centre of the bell curve in Figure 3.1 does not move to the left. In other words if we don't manage to mobilize a critical mass of people who Can, Know and Want to support the strategic change.

The obese-smoker syndrome

Many organizations focus mainly on the Know or in how far people cognitively understand the proposed change and are strategically aligned. Mobilizing for strategic change does undoubtedly involve a cognitive organizational reorientation. But it goes further and is beyond merely mobilizing minds. Many organizations still seem to suffer from the Obese Smoker Syndrome.[1] An obese smoker *knows* the strategy for more healthy living: stop smoking, eat less, and exercise regularly. In the same way 'just' knowing the proposed strategic change is not enough when it comes to mobilizing people. An obese smoker will go into action and change the status quo only when he or she *wants*. In other words mobilizing the hearts is of critical importance. We often focus our efforts on gaining a critical mass of people who are cognitively committed to the proposed strategic change. But they need to be affectively committed too! Affective commitment refers to employees' emotional attachment to, identification with, and involvement in making the organizational strategic change happen.[2] A critical mass of affective commitment amongst the workforce is the ultimate ingredient in making strategic change happen.

It should come as no surprise when a critical mass of people don't affectively embrace the proposed change based on being informed about it merely in a top-down manner. Here the executive team are seen as the sole architects of the projected strategic plan suggesting that the proposed strategy will overcome observed shortcomings. Too often we encounter such executive teams who spent a lot of time and effort on putting all kinds of information about their developed strategies in bulk emails, on web sites, in newsletters, through town-hall meetings or 'road shows'. The focus of such efforts are often too narrowly focussed on the Know and providing information behind the rationale of the developed strategic plan in particular. This informational approach typically does not allow for any possibility of alteration to the presented plan. The thinking behind this approach is that executive team needs to provide information and has to persuade the workforce to embrace the presented strategic plan. Such an approach too often fails to have the impact that executive teams desire. At best it may mobilize some people's minds but definitely not a critical mass of people's hearts. Research indicates that such a conventional approach will create significant energy for change in only about 20 per cent of the workforce.[3]

The power of collective dialogue and sensemaking

Strategic change becomes meaningful to people not just by getting to know the strategic plan but through dialogue and sensemaking of a wider story. The inconvenient truth according to a global consulting firm is that we are better off letting the workforce write their own story.[4] Typical executive teams invest a lot of time on 'communicating' the strategic change. But their efforts would be better spent listening, not telling. By not letting the workforce self-discover what the executive team already 'knows' it steals from them the energy needed to realize the change through a sense of 'owning the answers'.

Strategies by definition relate to change whether it is a change in direction, form, state, or function and therefore can be confronting for employees. Unknown or unexpected events tend to challenge established frames of reference and evoke uncertainty, ambiguity and fear.[5] People's existing frames of reference no longer suffice. So, it is important for people to have the opportunity to make sense of the new situation. This is done through 'sensemaking' or a narrative process by which people attribute meaning to unknown or unexpected events.[6] Sensemaking enables workforces to exchange their experiences and interpretations of such events. It is an important process in mobilizing a critical mass of the workforce because strategic change ultimately is dialogued into existence. Dialogue is the medium through which people seek shared meaning and understanding.[7] Facilitating dialogue among the workforce around strategic change is not something conventional leaders favour. Empirical research tells us that most organizations use a top-down approach to tell employees about the required strategic change.[8] Providing top-down information about what needs to be done seems easier than inviting a wide variety of reactions and interpretations. Instigating dialogue may initially be perceived as having to take a step backwards. But it is a worthwhile practice as the time and effort spent upfront actually enables taking two steps forward.

What we are not suggesting is endless deliberation sessions. Deliberation is closely related to dialogue but focuses more on decision taking through a collective process.[9] There is a difference between decision making and decision taking. What we are suggesting is for leaders to invite the perspectives of the wider workforce through dialogue as part of the strategic decision *making* process. Having considered the wider people's perspectives leaders then should be *taking* the strategic decisions as how best to move forward.

Scholars acknowledge the important role of dialogue leading to mobilization or collaborative action.[10] Dialogue not only increases sensemaking and the affective commitment of our people to the change but it also adds value through their enhancements of the originally proposed strategies. There can be different ways of seeing the same as discussed in the previous chapter and employees hold practical insights and wisdom that may not have been previously considered by the executive team. Through regular dialogue a cumulative practice can emerge where originally developed strategies move back and forth between leadership and groups of employees. By doing so, we improve both the quality of originally proposed change and affective buy-in from our people who will be implementing the strategies in the first place.

How do we instigate dialogue? By opening ourselves to dialogue we seek insights not just through our own eyes but also through others. We rely upon a leadership style that is perhaps more egalitarian rather than top-down. We acknowledge the limitations of being trapped in our own 'north view' and that any viewpoint is one among many. So, we are open to inviting a wider range of perspectives and seek feedback *throughout* the strategic change process.

We can instigate a dialogue only if we are genuinely interested in listening to our people, if we are willing to reflect upon perspectives different from our own and if we entertain the prospect of changing aspects of the original strategic plan by what we discover. Without an environment of trust and authenticity we risk having no more than a staged affectation.[11]

Making collective sense of seven 'simple' questions

No matter what the intended strategic change is it needs to be expressed through a *compelling story*. So, it goes beyond the specifics of the strategic plan itself. For people to make sense of the strategic plan it needs to be part of a wider and compelling story, which ultimately comprises seven 'simple' questions:

1. What are our desired behaviours?
2. Where have we come from?
3. Where are we today and what is our reason for being?
4. What does success look like by when?
5. How do we (need to) add value to whom?
6. What are our key focus areas and priorities?
7. What is your role in turning our story into reality?

On the surface these seven questions appear simple. But in practice we found that they are not easy to articulate and answer *collectively*. Starting with the leaders of an organization, we rarely come across executive teams who have a shared understanding and collectively can articulate all of these seven 'simple' questions. Sure each of the executive members will have his or her interpretation but they are often based on their individual 'north view' or own functional expertise and specific experiences.

The presented seven questions can form a compelling story for mobilizing the wider workforce for strategic change. Once the executive team themselves have a shared understanding of the seven questions then the story needs to be contextualized across the organization and made meaningful through the discussed sensemaking practices.

1 What are our desired behaviours?

The first 'simple' question relates to our shared values and behaviours. Everything in organizational life is values-driven and behavioural. There is little point initiating strategic change when people are not only aware of what the shared values are but when related desired behaviours are not consistently being demonstrated: especially by executives and management.

Organizational values refer to beliefs about standards of behaviour that people agree on demonstrating to achieve the organizational goals.[12] It is well understood that consistent demonstration of shared values through agreed behaviours provides a source of alignment, motivation, commitment and loyalty among the workforce.[13] Values represent the nucleus of an organization, the DNA of the culture if you like. All organizational behaviours orbit around values.

No organization will argue against the importance of values. Most organizations seem to have values but it goes beyond capturing a few pleasing words on a flip chart and then putting them on a mission statement. We do question the extent to which values have been embedded through behaviours that are then being demonstrated consistently and throughout the organization. Demonstration of values through agreed behaviours can be a huge mobilizing factor for people. As a key part in creating a compelling story people therefore need a behavioural point of reference. They need to know and demonstrate the values' related behaviours that are collectively deemed desirable. And stop the ones that are deemed undesirable...

Behaviours we need to Stop-Start-Continue

Yet many of us don't discuss what the behaviours are that we need to Stop, Start and Continue as part of our change story. When embarking on strategic change there should be an upfront agreement amongst the workforce and the leadership team as to what the desired behaviours are.

What are the behaviours we need to STOP within this team? This question we often ask members of executive teams for them to answer anonymously. It is not uncommon for them to identify the following behaviours that need to be stopped: silo-behaviour; being negative; self promotion; tolerating mediocrity; being cynical; excusing bad behaviour; being defensive of own patch; pretending to live the values; being reactive; working as an individual; being political;

competing against ourselves; missing deadlines; procrastination; blaming others; sitting on the fence; dwelling on the past; or being too operational. In several cases executives also identify bullying as a behaviour among colleagues that needs to be stopped. It raises the question: What are the chances of a compelling story being created, workforces being mobilized and strategic change being realized when such behaviours are demonstrated by members of the organization's leadership team?

It is perhaps not surprising when asking a typical leadership team to identify which behaviours they then need to START for them to identify: acting as one team; giving constructive feedback; sharing common objectives; better communication; actively recognizing each other; being collaborative; having open and honest conversations; promote uniformly; engaging in active listening; sharing of information, ideas and best practices; being empathetic; understanding each other's areas; celebrating collective successes; being transparent; and being more strategic.

By validating the findings of a team's Stop-Start-Continue exercise some generic themes can be identified and agreed as to what the desired behaviours are that need to be demonstrated collectively and individually going forward. A shared agreement on behaviours to be demonstrated is a critical first step. It becomes the organization's or team's ground rules or code of conduct so to speak. Such a collectively agreed behavioural conduct is an essential first step on embarking any strategic change program.

The six C's of desired behaviours

We believe there are six behavioural tenets that executive teams and their organizations need to demonstrate when embarking on strategic change. They are Collectiveness, Collaboration, Congruence, Cohesion, Compassion and Concurrency.

Collectiveness refers to the extent to which everyone in the entity strategically acts as a whole and is viewed as one. *Collaboration* considers the extent to which members work together towards co-creating and realizing the strategic change. It also considers the nature of the dialogue in which members determine together what the strategic priorities are and how best to action them.[14] *Congruence* refers to values-congruence or the homogeneity between individual and team or organizational values. It also refers to goal-congruence or the extent that individuals perceive their own goals as being satisfied by the accomplishment of the team's or organizational strategic goals. *Cohesion* is about team bonding and is what keeps any group together. It is about the level of affective connection to each other. *Compassion* relates to feelings of empathy to other members of the team. It is not merely understanding their qualms, fears or anguishes but feeling these as if you have experienced them yourself. Lastly, *Concurrency* considers the extent to which members of the team or organization step up at the same time to actively champion and lead the strategic change.

When embarking on strategic change, the described six C's can serve as a point of reference and represent the key drivers for bringing significant and positive outcomes to team and organizational behaviour.

2   Where have we come from?

The second 'simple' question to be answered collectively as part of our compelling story is *Where have we come from?* But strategy is about the future ... or is it? It is a misconception that the concept of strategy should look only toward the future. A purely future-facing orientation ignores powerful ground for thinking both that the past matters and that history is far from being an exclusively negative influence.[15]

We obviously can learn from the past and we want to avoid 'reinventing the wheel'. A shared understanding of the past provides us with the basis or platform from which to look into the future. Or as Confucius once stated 'study the past if you would define the future'. Looking back is of course easier than looking into the future since we do possess tangible data of our past.

By looking where we have come from it is valuable to have a shared understanding of 'what we have done well' and 'what we could have done better'. In the spirit of positive psychology we suggest not to start with the question 'What have we messed up in the last two years?' What we have done well collectively does not appear to be asked a lot. Organizational life always seems about moving forward faster and we forget to stand still and reflect on what actually has been achieved together.

We sometimes ask teams to think back and tell us what they feel they have done well in the past two years. We then put the mentioned deliverables on a white board and ask the team members for their reactions. They usually tell us that seeing their past accomplishments listed gives them a sense of achievement and pride. Needless to say that such moments need to be recognized. Recognition generically is the most important driver for people to continue exerting extra-energies.[16]

Without devaluing past performance it is notable that most listed achievements of typical leadership teams are internally focussed. More often than not they will bring up internally driven accomplishments such as completion of a restructure, roll-out of an IT system, recruitment of key staff, successful rebranding or launch of new website. What is often missing of such lists is the completion of novel and customer-centric activities or D-options.

This brings us to another important reason why it is valuable to be collectively aware of 'where we have come from' versus 'where we are today and where we need to go'. Referring to the analogies used in the previous chapter we may have worked on incremental A, B, or C strategies conveniently within our 'north view'. But D-options may now well be required to keep pace with our changing environment. Through a clear understanding of where we have come from we can ascertain in how far we are strategically drifting. Strategy Professor Hensmans and his colleagues describe strategic drift as the tendency for strategies to be developed incrementally on the basis of the dominant logic of businesses but failing to keep pace with a changing environment.[17] Problems may arise not because we fail to change per se but because the rate or nature of change of strategy lags behind the rate of change in our environment. Hensmans warns us that imperceptibly, taken-for-granted ways of seeing and doing things take root in an organization's culture. Core assumptions, organizational routines and structures and even the stories people tell each other all cohere to reinforce 'the way we do things around here'. The way we have been doing things around here may not suffice anymore. We cannot be captured by our past 'north view' as per our earlier analogy.

The overall lesson seems to be that we need to be able to see the past in relation to where we are today and where we need to go in the future. On the other hand we need to see what the future demands but does *not* require from the past.

3   Where are we today & what's our reason for being?

Having gained a shared understanding of what our desired behaviours are and where we have come from, the third 'simple' question of our compelling story relates to our present position. It can be split into two sub-questions. Firstly, 'What are our key threats, risks, challenges, and weaknesses that we are facing today?' Secondly, 'What is our shared purpose?'

Creating a positive burning platform

In gaining a shared understanding of where we are today, we firstly need to identify our key threats, risks, challenges and weaknesses that we are facing. Collective identification of these as part of our sensemaking practice can explain the reasons behind the required strategic change. It can serve as a 'burning platform' and collective call-to-action.

We have mixed feelings on how to create a burning platform as part of a compelling story. Too often a 'burning platform' is created and communicated in a conventional command-and-control fashion. This deficit-based approach is largely futile in mobilizing people. Research has shown that a relentless focus on 'what's wrong' is not sustainable, invokes blame, and creates change fatigue and resistance as cited by a global consulting firm.[18] In order to motivate and mobilize people we need to create an emotional story that enables strategic change. If people work in fear, they contract and retract and 'are in no place to experiment with new behaviours', suggests Marshall Ganz from Harvard University.[19]

This has led to the rise of 'appreciative inquiry', which is an approach that advocates collective inquiry into the best of what is in order to imagine what could be followed by collective design of a desired future state that is compelling.[20] Proponents of appreciate inquiry claim that their practice is based on the assumption that organizations are socially constructed. The practice seeks to create processes of inquiry that result in better, more effective, convivial, sustainable and vital social systems.[21]

We agree that (organizational) life is socially constructed. But it is also clear to us that a single-minded focus – on *either* what's wrong as per the deficit-based approach or on what's right as per the appreciate inquiry approach – is not the best way to mobilize people. Bluntly speaking we think an over-emphasis on the positive is unrealistic and some anxiety is good. Surely a 'burning platform' as an impetus for changing the status quo can be socially constructed – collectively and in a positive way. Making sense as how best to mitigate risks and turn challenges into opportunities can be done in a constructive and collective manner. It becomes an important sensemaking practice and part of our compelling story. Feelings of fear can naturally undermine the ability for strategic change. To counteract these emotions we need a story that still does address the urgency for change but yet sparks a sense of hope, purpose, efficacy and solidarity. All of these are affective states that enable people mobilization for strategic change.[22]

Do we have a shared purpose?

At this stage of our compelling story we are not talking about a *mission* but a *purpose*. Unlike the majority of practitioners and academics, we do differentiate between purpose and mission. We acknowledge that ours is a position that is rarely found in the literature except for Collins and Porras, who made a similar distinction.[23]

Simply put we believe that a good mission should answer the question: *What* do we do and *how* do we add value to *whom* with what kind of offering *where*? A mission is a strategic concentration that has to shift over a period of time as market and customer conditions change. Specific strategic missions have to change since external variables are changing constantly.

On the other hand a purpose explains the organization's fundamental reason for existence. An organizational purpose is more enduring and goes much deeper than a particular strategic mission. An organizational purpose typically outlasts planning cycles of developed visions, missions and strategic objectives. A shared and authentic purpose creates a deeper sense of meaning, identity and belonging for people as it encompasses the creation of not only organizational and customer value but typically also the creation of societal or environmental value. In other words, a shared purpose is critical because it offers people a wider and common sense of *why* the organization exists. It is an important distinction because 'why' creates motivation and motivation creates the exertion of extra-energies and the exertion of extra-energies creates mobilization and mobilization means action. This is the part where things often go wrong in our view. Many of the organizations we are exposed to find it hard to articulate a shared organizational purpose. Incidentally Collins and Porras could not find any explicit statements of purpose in the companies they researched either.[24] We believe there is little point introducing any future strategic change if we cannot articulate and embrace a shared purpose today as part of our compelling story. A shared and authentic purpose is a key enduring ingredient in installing genuine feelings of responsibility among people to help and take the organization forward.

4   What does success look like by when?

The fourth 'simple' question of our compelling story relates to the most critical aspect of leadership, namely to development and inculcation of a shared vision for the organization. In other words, what our preferred future is, what success looks like or what our strategic intent is? Although we will use these terms interchangeably we feel that a vision like a mission and purpose is more than just a statement. All too often statements of vision remain just that: statements. We would argue that the sensemaking practice of visioning is more important than the eventual vision statement itself. So, we prefer referring to the *practice of visioning*. We believe that the practice of visioning encompasses the following:

1. The initial and ongoing envisioning of an image of a desired future organizational state in the longer term, through;
2. Seeing, feeling and thinking about that desired state from the Outside-in, where;
3. The collective sensemaking of the vision serves to create a driving force for shared direction, cohesion and mobilization.

What *makes a vision we all can yearn for?*

The revered French writer Antoine de Saint-Exupéry once said, 'If you want to build a ship, don't drum up the men to gather wood, divide the work and give orders. Instead, teach them to yearn for the vast and endless sea'. So, what really makes a vision we all can yearn for?

First of all, we all realize that visioning is important because if we cannot collectively imagine what success looks like then how can we expect people to make any strategic change happen? Nothing mobilizes people more than having a shared vision we all can yearn for. When a vision is salient, people will view their participation as meaningful and important. It becomes part of their everyday actions, not a one-off activity or a fad for a month but a way of collective dreaming, raising the excitement level and focussing on the shared agenda, according to Lynda Gratton from London Business School.[25]

When the vision is not perceived to be compelling people will have less of a psychological and emotional stake in it and our overall strategic change story becomes feeble. In this case people's involvement may be the result of obligation rather than true enthusiasm. Moreover, if they feel that the strategic vision is inappropriate people are more apt to impede the design and implementation of strategy. This resistance can surface in the form of roadblocks to implementation, outright sabotage of the strategy or unnecessary delays in executing the strategy.[26]

Again what makes a compelling vision we all can yearn for? We already know that clichéd visions don't mobilize. We cannot expect people to go into-fifth-gear for mumbo-jumbo visions. The 'most successful', 'world's best', 'market-leading', 'best-in-class', 'best customer value', 'best customer experience', 'superior this and that' all mean nothing and will simply put people off!

We reiterate our belief that compelling visioning is unlocked from the Outside-In by seeing, feeling and thinking differently about the distinctive future value that we need to demonstrate. As discussed in Chapter 1 this originates from imaginative D-options beyond the reach of conventional thinking. The organizational vision needs to be distinctive and perceived by people as being relevant, inspirational, aspirational and attainable. Without these characteristics true strategic vision cannot be said to exist. It simply cannot exist without being meaningful by a critical mass of the workforce.

Who *makes a vision we all can yearn for?*

It is difficult to argue against the effectiveness of visionary and charismatic leaders in mobilizing their people for change. We only need to think of the impact of visionary humanitarian leaders like Nelson Mandela, Mahatma Gandhi and Martin Luther King. Or visionary corporate leaders like Henry Ford, Walt Disney, Bill Gates and Steve Jobs. The stereotype of such corporate leaders is an individual of great vision who inspires his or her people to heroic acts of performance. Like the stereotype of the lone genius who develops a paradigm-changing innovation, it is a romantic perspective but not one which bears a great deal of resemblance for the majority of organizations out there.

The described stereotype where vision is embodied specifically by the leader is called *visionary leadership*.[27] Most organizations have evolved to what we would like to call (executive) *team visioning* realizing that teams are stronger than individuals; teams are wiser than individuals; teams are more resilient than individuals; teams are more adventurous than individuals; teams are more creative than individuals; and teams are more capable than individuals.[28] The myth of the lone visionary leader is exactly that and even when an executive team is not formally involved in the visioning, an informal network of minds is often contributing to it anyway. Regardless of how distinctive the created vision is, it generally is difficult for a lone visionary leader to mobilize the whole organization without being surrounded by a team of 'disciples' co-owning and spreading the vision.

However, we feel that visioning can be enhanced further by moving from team visioning to true *organizational visioning*. Many executive teams are often trapped in their own loop of inference or the 'north view' paradigm as described in the previous chapter. In our search for both a distinctive vision and a critical mass of people supporting that vision, why not involve the wider organization in the co-creation of the vision? This is exactly what Collins and Porras suggested about a quarter of a century ago.[29] They argued that a company's vision should not be set just by the CEO nor the executive team but at all levels and throughout the company. The creation of the organizational vision should not only involve all levels of an organization but each group should set its own vision consistent of course with the overall vision of the corporation. Collins and Porras wondered what if there is no overall vision from above that can be latched onto? All the more reason to do so as they observed situations where middle management initiated its own vision-setting process and then virtually demanded that the executives of the company do the same for the entire organization.

As pointed out earlier in this chapter we propose for leaders to invite the perspectives not just of the immediate executive team but also of the wider workforce through dialogue as part of the visioning decision *making* practice. Having considered the wider people's perspectives leaders then should be *taking* the decisions as how best to move forward.

5 How do we (need to) add value to whom?

Having a shared understanding of what our desired behaviours are, where we have come from, where we are today and what success looks like, the fifth 'simple' question of our compelling story relates to what our mission is.

Not another clichéd mission statement

Question: What do the 25 mission statements in Figure 3.2 have in common?

Answer: They are all full of fluff, not specific enough, no differentiation, internally driven, and full of jargon. In short not inspiring and compelling. We analysed the mission statements of *Fortune* 500 companies and we limited ourselves to highlighting the 25 examples of clichéd mission statements as illustrated in Figure 3.2. We probably could have extended the list by a few hundred. With such a large number of uninspiring mission statements it is perhaps not surprising that the average lifespan of the top 500 leading US companies has decreased by more than 50 years in the past century to just 15 years today, according to Professor Richard Foster from Yale University.[30]

By taking a closer look at the *Fortune* 500 mission examples in Figure 3.2 we can see that the main drivers behind mission statements 1–4 is to become 'the leader', which arguably sounds more like a bad vision statement. The main drivers for mission statements 5–7 are 'increasing shareholder value' and 8–10 is 'maximizing profit'. All of the ten statements indistinctly describe the ultimate effect. Of course we all want to become leaders, increase shareholder value and maximize profits. But what are the customer-centric value propositions behind these outcomes that should describe our true mission ultimately resulting in us 'becoming leaders and increasing shareholder value and profits'? Mission statements 11–14 are mostly internally driven and about 'excellence and efficiencies'. The companies behind mission statements 15–17 have begun to realize that the ultimate reason for being should perhaps start with the customer. Unfortunately they don't articulate in their statements how their company actually adds value other than futile jargons like 'delighting everyone' and 'outstanding service'. The *Fortune* 500 companies behind mission statements 18–23 decided to be 'the best in everything

1. Undisputed marketplace leadership
2. To be the leader in every market we serve to the benefit of our customers and our shareholders
3. To be the premier provider of targeted specialized insurance products and related services in North America and selected other markets
4. To be the performance leader achieving operational excellence, industry-leading customer satisfaction and superior financial performance
5. To deliver a competitive and sustainable rate of return to shareholders
6. Create value for shareholders through the energy business
7. To build value for our investors through the strength of our customers' satisfaction and by consistently producing superior operating results
8. To grow profitably in the world's vehicular markets and provide industry-leading shareholder value
9. Profitable growth through superior customer service, innovation, quality and commitment
10. To be America's best-run, most-profitable automotive retailer
11. To deliver operational excellence in every corner of the Company and meet or exceed our commitments to the many constituencies we serve
12. To set standards of excellence with regard to environmental matters
13. To be the most efficient and innovative global provider of semiconductor solutions
14. We add value with efficient and cost-effective service and solutions for our customers and our suppliers
15. To nourish and delight everyone we serve
16. To supply outstanding service and solutions through dedication and excellence
17. To provide products and services to the market which meet or exceed the reasonable expectations of our customers. Satisfying our customers with the appropriate level of quality is a primary goal and a fundamental element of our business mission
18. To be the best in the eyes of our customers, employees and shareholders
19. To serve our customers, employees, shareholders and society by providing a broad range of staffing services and products
20. One company, one team, one goal: creating superior value for our customers, employees, partners, and shareholders
21. To create superior value for our customers, employees, communities and investors through the production, conversion, delivery and sale of energy and energy services
22. To be our customers' favourite place and way to eat and drink. Our worldwide operations are aligned around a global strategy called the Plan to Win, which centre on an exceptional customer experience – People, Products, Place, Price and Promotion. We are committed to continuously improving our operations and enhancing our customers' experience
23. We are a market-focused, process-centred organization that develops and delivers innovative solutions to our customers, consistently outperforms our peers, produces predictable earnings for our shareholders, and provides a dynamic and challenging environment for our employees
24. Our mission is positive outcomes
25. To unlock the potential of nature to improve the quality of life

Figure 3.2   Selection of clichéd mission statements of *Fortune* 500 companies

to everybody' ending up with saying a lot about nothing. Finally, the companies behind statements 24 and 25, well ...

Beyond Management-101

How can we mobilize people for future strategic change if we don't have a compelling and shared mission? At the end of the day we need a shared articulation of one single and 'simple' question as part of our story representing the mission:

> What do we do and how do we add value to whom with what kind of proposition where?

It seems like a basic question within a Management-101 course. But the danger is in the perceived simplicity of the question. In answering this question we don't simply ask to list what we produce or the services we offer from an internally driven perspective as clichéd mission statements do. One could argue that 'half the world' could be offering similar products or services. A company's employees don't really need to be told that the mission of XYZ Widgets is to make the best widgets in the world while providing excellent service. As opposed to what? Making the worst widgets and offering the lousiest service?[31] Such clichéd statements don't contribute to a compelling story but point out that leadership lacks imagination and perhaps in some cases direction.

So, we reject the conventional assumption that a mission statement merely defines the organization's primary objectives where its prime function is internal to define the key measures of the organization's success and its prime audience is the leadership and its shareholders. A mission is not simply a statement about describing what we do for financial gains and for whom. That is not compelling enough.

A good mission is constructed from the Outside-In addressing how we *add value* to whom. It goes beyond merely describing what we offer. There are no shortcuts, no silver bullets, no gimmicks that can replace the reality of the marketplace – ultimately demonstrating customer value wins. So, how do we add value to our customers and how do we demonstrate that value? What are our points of differentiation? What makes our offerings unique so that customers stay with us?

Still too many organizations don't know what really differentiates them from their competition. In one of his blogs Richard Branson refers to the mission statement for the pharmaceutical giant Bristol-Myers that reads *To discover, develop and deliver innovative medicines that help patients prevail over serious diseases.* Well, you can't argue with that but surely this can be said of every drug company on the planet. Why would a person choose to buy Bristol-Myers' products or invest in its stock rather than its competitors'?[32]

In the same spirit we question Kaplan and Norton who gave us an example of what they called an 'excellent' mission statement in their book *The Execution Premium* (2008). The Balanced Scorecard originators referred to the 'excellent' mission statement from yet another pharmaceutical giant Merck: *To provide society with superior products and services by developing innovations and solutions that improve the quality of life and satisfy customer needs, and to provide employees with meaningful work and advanced opportunities, and investors with a superior rate of return.*[33] We question the 'excellence' of this mission statement as it does not differentiate anything. Ironically by 2014 Merck had changed their mission to be almost identical to the earlier mentioned and indifferent one of Bristol-Myers: *To discover, develop and provide innovative products and services that save and improve lives around the world.*[34]

In search of a meaningful mission

IKEA's mission offers us a great example of a truly customer-centric statement. It doesn't talk about being the leader, increasing shareholder value, maximizing profits, being excellent and efficient, delighting our customers nor being the best in everything to everyone. Instead their mission or what they call 'business idea' is all about *offering a wide range of well-designed, functional home furnishing products at prices so low that as many people as possible will be able to afford them.*[35] Importantly they then *quantify* each of the added value 'promises' within the overall statement by letting us know as *how* they do it. They describe the distinctiveness of their product range, materials used, design and function, low prices, and the flat packing saving shipping costs not to mention their responsibility to people and the environment. They even describe how they see things differently. IKEA understands that by delivering on their customer-centric mission consistently and sustainably the ultimate effects or outcomes will be a leadership position with increased customer satisfaction and profits.

Without getting too philosophical about it we do acknowledge that articulating *how we are adding value to whom with what kind of proposition where* compellingly and collectively is not easy. Many leadership teams find it hard to *collectively* articulate their mission in this format. What we found is that team members often articulate their own interpretation of a reason for being based on their individual 'north view' or own functional perspective and beliefs. Not a united one. But the point we are making is that it really becomes difficult to mobilize people for strategic change when there is no collective understanding and affective engagement with our mission.

If all fails perhaps we can take advice from Richard Branson,[36] who says that brevity is key. Branson advises to try using Twitter's 140-character template when you are drafting your inspirational message. You need to explain your company's mission by making it unique to your company, making it memorable and just for fun imagine it on the bottom of a coat of arms. If we had to put ours on a coat of arms Virgin's would probably say something like *Ipsum sine timore, consector,* which very loosely translated from the Latin means *Screw it, let's do it!*

6 What are our key focus areas and priorities?

The sixth 'simple' question relates to our priorities for the short to medium term as part of our strategic plan to realizing the vision. For our change story to be compelling the strategic plan needs to be succinct, prioritized, balanced and created from different perspectives.

There is no point trying to make sense of – or execute for that matter – twenty-plus strategic objectives within a 70-page or so strategic document full of analysis and mumbo jumbo. We should limit the number of strategic objectives to a maximum of seven. We believe that a higher number of strategic objectives becomes overwhelming for people and difficult to communicate, remember and focus on. The prioritized strategic objectives need to have been developed from different but interrelated perspectives for our plan to be balanced.

Any organization needs a sense of where it should be heading from a *financial* perspective. Fortunately most of us have no problems with creating financial growth objectives. But we often encounter that the proposed numbers simply don't add up. How are we going to grow revenue without increasing cost for example? The strategy might look great but what investments are we putting behind it? So, without devaluing the need for thorough financial strategies it should also be appreciated that such financial 'targets' are internally driven and are the ultimate effect or outcome. What is much more difficult to create are the underlying strategies from a *customer* perspective that ultimately then result in the strategized financial outcomes.

Besides creating strategies from financial and customer perspectives we also need to create strategies from an *internal support* perspective. Questions to ask here are what the required processes, systems, technologies, tools, infrastructure, business model, policies and procedures are for our customer objectives to be enabled. Internal support strategies clearly are important but caution should be taken not to create too many such objectives. Internal support objectives such as overhauling certain IT systems are often extremely resources, time, and capital intensive. It is not uncommon for organizations to be caught up in such internally focussed change projects often at the cost of realizing customer objectives.

The ultimate enabling factor of all created financial, customer and internal support strategies is of course our *people*. It is like cause and effect. If we don't create meaningful people strategies our customer, internal support, and subsequently financial objectives will not be realized. In other words, this whole process has become yet another theoretical exercise. So, regardless of what kind of specific strategy 'pillars' or methodology we prefer our strategies need to be created at least from the four described perspectives as they all are inter-linked. If any of the four is missing our strategic plan is not balanced.

Depending on the nature of the organization additional perspectives should be considered. Strategic objectives may need to be created from certain stakeholders' perspectives like communities, government, trade unions, investors, owners, and suppliers. Other perspectives may include Corporate Social Responsibility or Health Safety and Environment, particularly in manufacturing.

7 What is your role in turning our story into reality?

The last 'simple' question of our compelling story for strategic change relates to the individual or 'me'. What is my particular role and how can I contribute? So, it is important to make clear to people that the organizational strategy will be contextualized at the divisional, departmental and team levels. An organizational strategy per definition is broad and can only come to life when it is meaningful, not only at the various levels of the organization, but especially at individual level.

In summary, making strategic change happen is truly a people's game. People are the ultimate enabling factor in moving from strategic plans to enduring execution. So, it is beyond just informing people of the specifics of the strategic plan. It is about dialogue and collectively making sense of the strategic change through the described seven 'simple' questions that make up our compelling story:

1. What are our desired behaviours?
2. Where have we come from?
3. Where are we today and what is our reason for being?
4. What does success look like by when?
5. How do we (need to) add value to whom?
6. What are our key focus areas and priorities?
7. What is your role in turning our story into reality?

We feel that none of these questions can be left unanswered as it will jeopardize the support for the overall strategic change program. For people to start exerting extra-energies on top of their day-to-day operational challenges and support the change they will need to personally identify with the organization's values, behaviours, purpose, vision, mission and not just the proposed strategic plan. People will support the strategic change only when they can identify with the overall story so that the co-created change is no longer seen by an individual employee as separate from the self.

4
Co-Creating Distinctive Strategies

The first problem arises from confusing strategic planning with strategy development. How many more times do we hear 'we need to create a strategic plan' as opposed to 'we need to create a strategy'? This is because most people see strategy as an exercise in producing a planning document. In this conception, strategy is manifested as a long to-do-list with actions, timings and accountabilities. Indeed strategic planning is about prioritizing developed strategic objectives and linking them to quantifiable actions, measurements, timings and accountabilities. A common mistake many of us make is to try and actually *develop* strategies during a periodic strategic planning session. But the key ingredients for developing distinct strategies are insights. Such insights rarely emerge from strategic planning sessions as highlighted in a *Harvard Business Review* article.[1] Yet almost 70 per cent of executives conduct strategic planning only at prescribed times; no wonder that only 11 per cent of executives feel that strategic planning is worth the effort.[2]

So, the answer to creating distinctive strategies is not periodic planning processes or better designed strategic plans. The focus should be less on action plans or even the articulation of the strategy itself but more on unlocking insights. Trying to create distinctive strategies without insights during an annual strategic planning session leads to unrealistic plans. The answer lies in unlocking these insights through strategic sensing or seeing, feeling and thinking differently and continuously as explored in Chapter 2.

Beyond conventional planning

In our quest to (co) creating distinctive strategies we need to undertake strategic sensing. For most of us this automatically means a SWOT analysis. But starting with our own perceived strengths, weaknesses, opportunities, and threats can be limiting as it is internally driven or at best from the Inside-Out. So, we recommend analysis that starts more at a macro-level and from the Outside-In. The first question to ask is what are the key external variables that impact on our organization? Answering this question leads us to building a comprehensive and continuously changing picture around political, economic, social, technological, environmental and legal or regulatory variances. The second level down involves analysis of markets, customers, new entrants, substitutes, suppliers, and competitors.

Incidentally we are often surprised with the limited insights that managers possess about direct, indirect, and potential competitors. A common failing in many organizations we engage with is failure to deeply understand the competition. One of the problems with trying to create distinct strategies is the lack of competitive intelligence. What are our competitors doing? How can we beat them? If strategy, in its original war context, is about 'terminating the enemy' and in its traditional business context is about 'competitive advantage' we would expect more time and resources to be allocated to competitor analysis. Yet we don't seem to scrutinize our competitors enough. Seeing and thinking differently about 'competitors' could in some cases even highlight that the competition is coming from our own suppliers or customers.[3]

The final level of analysis should then involve an organizational exploration in the form of a SWOT analysis. In the spirit of Chapter 2, all of the above-described strategic analyses are less relevant if conducted mainly from our 'north view'. We clearly want to avoid merely going through the exercise in order to 'test our own hypotheses' or specifically look for answers to our own predetermined questions. Another challenge with strategic analysis is the balance between analysing all variables and creating timely strategies. Clearly, we don't want to spend so much time analysing that when it comes to the actual implementation 'the goal posts have moved on'.

Beyond monopolized planning

Another misconception held by many executives is not only the belief that distinctive strategies can be developed during a periodic planning session but that they are to be formulated mainly by *them*. This wrongly assumes that the organizational strategy is something that should be developed and planned for by executives well in advance and then to be executed by the workforce. But by doing so organizational leaders monopolize strategy formulation by excluding certain key internal *and* external stakeholders. For instance, around the executive team *who* represents the insights of key implementers who often aren't involved in the formulation yet are still expected to understand the reasoning behind the strategy and make it all happen? This is often a missing link between strategy formulation and strategy implementation as identified by various researchers.[4] Around the executive team who possesses to represent the required *deep* insights, for instance, of customers, of the workforce, of communities, of the board and of other stakeholders? How can distinctive strategies be developed mostly in isolation of such important stakeholders?

So, the notion that distinctive strategies can be developed mainly by leaders during a scheduled planning session once or twice a year is totally out of step with our rapidly changing world.[5] The approach and output of what we call a *continuous strategy practice* is quite different (see Figure 4.1).

Conventional strategic planning	Continuous strategy practice
• Traditional strategic thinking	• Seeing, feeling and thinking differently
• Strategies driven from Inside-Out	• Strategies co-created from Outside-In
• Periodic planning	• Continuous practice
• Executive development of the strategic plan	• Co-creation of a compelling story
• Sequential or incremental strategy development	• Emergent strategy co-creation
• Top-down information or communication	• Collective dialogue and sensemaking
• Aim is proficiency, understanding and alignment (Can and Know)	• Aim is Can, Know & Want (affective commitment and strategic engagement)
• Process focussed	• Behavioural driven

Figure 4.1 From periodic strategic planning to continuous strategy practice

Under our proposed continuous practice, the concept of strategy isn't just about occasional planning cycles where executives develop the organization's strategies. It is not about leaders coming up with all the answers. But it is about leaders making possible different practices continuously. It is about leaders driving continuous practices of seeing, feeling and thinking differently from the Outside-In where strategies are co-created with internal and external stakeholders involving collective dialogue and sensemaking.

Frankly, there is nothing new about this phenomenon. More than two decades ago scholars highlighted that strategic innovation occurs through combining different insights and knowledge bases.[6] They pointed out that organizations need to nurture their ability to create, integrate and recombine insights that come from different contributors inside *and* outside their traditionally perceived boundaries.

Co-creating internally with the executive team and the workforce has already been explored in the previous chapter. Before we look at co-creating strategies outside our traditionally perceived boundaries with external stakeholders we first explore co-creating with other internal stakeholders such as the board and 'internal outsiders'. We use the terms 'strategy development', 'strategy formulation' and 'strategy creation' interchangeably.

Co-creating with the board

The board seems an obvious choice for an executive team to involve in co-creating the organizational strategy. The independent perspective, long-term focus and experience-fuelled wisdom of board members can represent an invaluable asset. A variety of perspectives can be promoted and explored in particular when the board composition is diversified. But there seems to be much confusion among CEOs and board members regarding a board's role in the development of the organization's strategy. Is the board responsible for creating the organisational strategy or is this overstepping the mark?

Frankly we have got mixed thoughts about the role of the board when it comes to strategy creation. This could be perceived as a challenging point of view especially after proclaiming the desired involvement of different perspectives of various stakeholders in co-creating strategies. Whilst we are not contesting that the board has a role to play when it comes to strategy creation we don't want to lose sight of who ultimately should be driving the creation of the organizational strategy. That has to be the CEO and his or her executive team. Otherwise why have an executive team? Surely, creation and execution of the organizational strategy is the prime function of an executive leadership team. Yet we observe some boards 'demanding' a leading role in strategy creation especially when they lack confidence in the capabilities of the executive team. But if the board were to be unhappy with the quality of the proposed organizational strategies as presented by the executive team then the board's focus should be on fixing the CEO and his or her executive team.

Too far down in the weeds

The strategic capability of many boards themselves is in question. Despite the increased economic volatility requiring more and better board engagement with the organizational strategy it actually doesn't come easy to them.[7] This provocative finding is based on a majority of board directors admitting to their own strategic shortcomings in various surveys. A survey conducted by the National Association of Corporate Directors (NACD) in the US found that less than 20 per cent of respondents rated their boards as highly effective at strategy even though they rated it the most important issue to board governance.[8] In a previous survey, the NACD revealed that whilst CEOs gave a top ranking to the importance of board participation in strategy, they ranked the actual effectiveness of their Boards in strategy only number 11.[9] In a McKinsey survey of board directors, only one in five claimed to have a complete understanding of the current strategy and only one in ten felt they fully understood the industry dynamics in which their companies operated.[10]

These findings are perhaps not surprising when realizing that only half of public companies discuss strategy at every board meeting. And, they only meet between four and seven times a year.[11] During such meetings the level of debate often is not strategic but merely operational downloads where we do observe board members too far down in the weeds. On the other hand, board members often do wish to raise the level of strategic debate with the executive team but complain that strategy presentations by executives are too rehearsed and just information dumps without an opportunity for deeper dialogue.[12]

The described challenges together with increased economic volatility should prompt organizations to rethink their strategic rhythm. It should become less calendar driven and formulaic. Instead, it should become a co-creational journey involving regular dialogue among and between the board and the executive team. Strategy is a living organism, which is constantly evolving and therefore demands continuous engagement. Not just during half of the periodic board meetings or an annual strategy workshop.

For organizations to remain relevant, boards must join executive teams on this co-creational journey and executive teams in turn must bring the board along. All, while ensuring that strategic co-creation doesn't become confusion, or worse, shadow management.[13] Too many boards are indeed shadow managing where their role in formulating strategy is simply reviewing and approving the executive team's proposed strategy.[14]

Boards who Can-Know-Want

A precursor to realizing the benefits from co-creating strategies is a critical mass of board members who Can, Know, and Want. So, the first imperative is to recruit and retain board members with the right skills and competencies who CAN engage in high-value strategic dialogue and decision-making. The second imperative is for collective board members to KNOW the organization's industry. Sure, it is beneficial to have out-of-industry experience. But as it stands only one in ten board members fully understands the industry dynamics in which their own companies operate as indicated in the earlier McKinsey survey. Not surprisingly industry knowledge tops the list of type of skill or experience most desired for board success as researched by Deloitte.[15] The third imperative requires board members to be passionate about strategy. We may have board members who Can and Know but do they WANT to exert extra-energies to help realize strategic change? Are they willing and able to invest time on a more continuous basis? Commitment and ownership are essential factors.

So, whether we have the right board members who Can, Know, and Want to co-create and oversee the next strategy iteration becomes a fundamental question. We believe that the board should be evaluated the same way the executive team is. If board members are not the right people to co-create and oversee strategic change, we need new board members.

Aligning board and CEO and executive team

There can be a number of benefits to co-creating strategies with a capable board. Firstly, it facilitates the tapping of wider insights likely resulting in the creation of more meaningful strategies. Secondly, alignment and buy-in is more likely to be gained. There should be no surprises and all noses of both the members of the board *and* the executive team should be pointing in the same direction. Thirdly, the practice builds strong ownership and support from the board. A reservoir of goodwill is being created that is particularly useful when the organization hits a difficult period or crises. A board that has been engaged is much more likely to support the executive team in times of dire need because it understands that its support is truly deserved.[16]

So, there is a more active role to play for boards without them *driving* the strategy creation. Whilst the CEO and executive team lead strategy development they should seek the board's insights and input *throughout* the process. This can also be done informally. Wise CEOs spend at least 30 minutes with each board member every quarter just to go through the organizational strategy together.

In addition to the organizational strategy being formally discussed at *every* board meeting and the CEO updating each board member on a frequent basis, we do recommend collaborative strategic off-sites. The objective of such off-sites is not necessarily to actually develop strategic objectives but to realign the board, CEO, and executive team around: 1) What we have done well and what we could have done better during the past 12 months? 2) What our current risks, challenges, threats, and weaknesses are? 3) Whether our purpose is still relevant? and 4) What success looks like by when, for instance, from financial, market & customer, internal support, and people perspectives. Once re-alignment is reached around these four key strategic questions, the CEO and executive team can go and co-create the specific strategic objectives and actions required.

Co-creating with internal outsiders

In our quest for different insights and creating distinctive strategies we also need to look beyond the executive leadership team and the board. We need to invite different paradigms to our own by inviting a very different kind of insiders. One way of doing this is by identifying and involving a critical mass of *internal outsiders* with the creation of the organizational strategy.

Internal outsiders are non-mainstream thinkers or across-the-grain thinkers or perhaps mavericks. They are people already within the organization who see, feel and think differently. *Internal outsiders transform tradition-bound organizations* according to the authors of an identically titled journal article.[17] According to the authors, internal outsiders may be located in diverse functions, business units and levels. They typically come from second- and third-level management. They may be in subsidiaries, headquarters or recently acquired organizations. By combining insiders from the periphery with insiders from the centre it stimulates very different ideas that can prove very effective with the co-creation *and* the implementation of distinct strategies.

Mobilizing the 'crazy' ones

The above-mentioned authors point out that it is a matter of proactively seeking internal outsiders out, giving them space and responsibility, and empowering them within a strategic task force. Sponsors of a strategic task force must dare to deviate from traditional profiles when filling the positions, as the role of an internal outsider is not a comfortable one. The fact that the internal outsider, the organizational deviant, the individual who sees, feels and thinks differently may be the vital link to a new and more apt paradigm, does not typically make an organization value such a person more. Most organizations would rather risk obsolescence than make room for the non-conformists in their midst.[18] But these are the 'crazy' ones who need seeking out. Or, as Steve Jobs said: 'Here's to the crazy ones, the misfits, the rebels, the troublemakers, the round pegs in the square holes... the ones who see things differently – they're not fond of rules... You can quote them, disagree with them, glorify or vilify them but the only thing you can't do is ignore them because they change things... they push the human race forward and while some may see them as the crazy ones, we see genius because the ones who are crazy enough to think that they can change the world are the ones who do'.[19]

Referring to some of the analogies used in the previous chapters, internal outsiders look at the world from the Outside-In and are capable of seeing 'D-options' that contradict established 'north views'. In other words, they are capable of looking at options from perspectives that differ from the one that is typically dominating the organization. The fact that they see different options that contradict the conventional 'wisdom' of the organization, doesn't mean that internal outsiders do not care or aren't loyal. Quite the opposite as they are concerned to the point that they need to speak out. By daring to speak out against established perspectives shows us that internal outsiders do care. It would be far easier for them to conform with the status quo. Instead, they are willing to open up to tackle the status quo and encourage strategic change for the organization.

The care factor in terms of wanting to realize strategic change for the betterment of the wider organization is a critical one. Internal outsiders are not to be confused with self-serving loners. Few people are willing to support self-serving loners. Workforces may be willing to sacrifice their day-to-day operational focus if they feel that the proposed change will result in a significant positive effect for the community with which they identify. In order for internal outsiders to attract allies people must perceive that a deep-seated commitment to the good of the wider organization is the central value and driving force for the strategic change.[20]

Sure, internal outsiders are necessary for helping co-create novel strategies. But they can't do this on their own. A culture of cooperation is crucial because internal outsiders alone cannot put enough in motion to achieve truly significant strategic change. Regardless of the distinctiveness of the created strategies. Gaining cooperation among the organization through dialogue and sensemaking as explored in the previous chapter provides an opportunity for the task force to identify allies and draw them together cooperatively.

Bring back the mavericks!

Now more than ever we need internal outsiders or mavericks in co-creating distinct strategies. Are they still around in our organizations? Mavericks may be perceived as a nice-to-have during good times. But we often don't realize that they can be vital game changers in times of downturn. Unfortunately, in today's quest for lean-and-mean organizational structures, we observe many internal outsiders becoming easy targets and victims of organizational 'restructuring' programs. It seems easier getting rid of the 'round pegs in the square holes' than the steady operational conformists. The strategic mistake many of us make when things are tough is to contract and retract to what we traditionally know. We often fail to realize that it is especially during times of downturn that we need to see, feel and think differently. This is achieved more likely through identifying, embracing and mobilizing internal outsiders rather than by exiting them.

Co-creating with customers

How are our *customers* informing the organizational strategy? It seems such a foolish question as in theory we would assume that our customers are the starting point of all our thinking and actions. But too many organizational strategies are still being created without real input and deep insights of our customers. How much time are we really spending with key customers, listening to their needs, trying to understand what success looks like for them and what their priorities are? Or, at least validating our developed strategies with them. After having created customer strategies how many of us actually go back to our key customers to validate what we have come up with?

The outcomes of just validating created strategies can be staggering. When validating with key customers it is not unusual to discover significant variances between what has been developed by the executive team and the actual strategic priorities as perceived by the customers. We have observed instances where executive teams invited key customers to validate the created 'innovative solutions' only for the customer to turnaround and disclose 'forget your 'innovative solution' we don't feel you are delivering on your core promises to us'. Such validation and feedback are invaluable because it means that it becomes of strategic importance to get our 'backyard' in order again so that we consistently and sustainably deliver on original customer promises. In such instances, it can occur especially in a business-to-business context that our customers don't even wish to co-create distinct 'D-options' because we have failed to demonstrate value through our core offering in the first place.

So, our customer strategies are not always as customer centric as we may assume. Underlying reasons may well be *the manner* in which we create customer strategies, our *main driver* for creating customer strategies, and the *level of involvement* of our customers in creating our strategies.

Three ways of creating customer strategies

There probably are three ways of creating *customer* strategies as part of the organizational strategy as illustrated in Figure 4.2.

The most basic and conventional way is *Inside creation*, where strategies are developed mainly in isolation of customers. This approach is not customer centric but internal and products driven. Customers are traditionally perceived as 'targets' and as passive recipients of our products or services. The relationship is transactional and our main driver is simply to increase sales. Once in a while we undertake a customer satisfaction survey as the main source of our insights.

A slightly improved approach is *Inside-Out creation*, where strategies are still mainly developed from an internal perspective. This approach still relies on what we traditionally think our customers need. Our source of insights are based largely on periodic surveys and mining our CRM database. Whilst many of us feel we are developing all kind of 'customer centric' offerings, in reality such strategies are often driven and created from the Inside-Out. Such strategies don't really involve our customers as they are created *for*, not *with*

	Inside strategy creation	Inside-Out strategy creation	Outside-In strategy co-creation
Nature of strategy creation	Strategies developed in isolation of customers	Strategies developed *for* customers	Strategies co-created together with customers
Main strategic driver	Increasing sales of products offered	Maximising company's value through optimizing current resources	Leveraging joint value through customer co-creation
Role of customer	Customer perceived as passive recipient of products	Reactive – customer as input in 'validating' new products	Active – customer as a competent partner in co-creating strategies
View on customers	Customers perceived as targets	Customers perceived mainly as stand-alone	Customers perceived as individuals (and members of social networks)
Nature of relationship	Simply transactional	Relationship building	Collaboration for joint co-creation of experience-based value
Source of insight	Mainly quantitatively based i.e. surveys	Mainly mining the Customer Relationship Management database	Gaining insights (virtually) with customers as well as expanding these together
Nature of interaction	On contingent basis and mainly one-way	On a periodic basis and mainly one-way	Continuous back and forth dialogue and sensemaking

Figure 4.2   Differences in creating customer strategies

our customers. An example is given by the authors of a recent article titled *Strategy and Co-Creation Thinking* by referring to self-checkout scanners at supermarkets or self-check-in kiosks at airports.[21] They argue that in such examples of customer 'involvement' the organization is still in charge of the overall or orchestration of the experience. The original thinking behind such strategies is often driven from the inside pursuing internal cost-savings rather than from the outside and in pursuit of true customer value. Many of such strategic offerings barely touch on the customers' potential to add value by shaping their own experience. So, traditionally we tend to develop strategies that optimize and maximize our own 'resources'. We ask ourselves whether we can do more and better with what we have got. But in this mental model the notion of optimizing and maximizing resources still remains internally motivated and confined to our organization. Why be limited by the internal focus on our current resources and capabilities or on 'what we have got'? Why not create strategies from an external or customer perspective first? Ergo why not co-discover and co-create strategic offerings *together* with our customers that are of true meaning to them? Such co-created strategies then become our 'size-of-the-prize' from which we can address the various (dis) enabling factors to making it happen. The shift we are encouraging is from an internal and resources-driven perspective to a true customer-centric one leveraging value through co-discovery and co-creation.

So, we advocate from the *Outside-In*, where strategies are co-created together with existing, new and prospective customers. In this externally centric practice, the aim is to leverage joint value through co-discovering deep insights and co-creating distinctive strategies together with our customers. Insights are gained as part of a continuous practice of dialogue and sensemaking both qualitatively and virtually.

Co-creating with mass-consumers

Henri Ford once said, 'If I had asked people what they wanted, they would have said faster horses'.[22] This is an old sentiment that even today seems to 'warrant' creating customer strategies that are mostly internally driven or at best from the Inside-Out. The reason being that we think we know best what our customers need. True, our customers don't always know what they need or want. They 'don't know what they don't know' so to speak. Most of us perhaps didn't know we 'needed' a third or fourth device when Apple launched the iPad in 2010.

But we are not back in 1908 when the first black Ford Model T was produced. Today our consumers are in the driving seat. 'Today the customer is in charge and whoever is best at putting the customer in charge makes all the money', according to a Wal-Mart Senior Vice President.[23] Today we are indeed in the middle of a consumer revolution that is dramatically changing – not only the way we manufacture, market, sell, and deliver our products and services but also the way we create our consumer strategies. It is a significant shift in strategy creation and one that many of us will need to adapt to quickly with the rising influence of mass-consumer communities.

So, the process of strategy creation is shifting away from a company- and product-centric perspective to a consumer-centric and community experience-based perspective where value is co-created. The increasing role that consumer communities will play not only in product validation but also in strategy creation cannot be underestimated. Digital technologies have dramatically opened the way to a deeper and wider consumer involvement.[24] Online consumer communities already have proved to be well organized and have become a powerful instrument in shaping relationships with organizations and their brands.[25] Such online aggregations or 'electronic tribes' are based on shared enthusiasm for – or dissatisfaction with – a product, issue or activity.

Online communities not only engage with organizations but importantly among themselves. They increasingly engage in dialogue with peers or 'consumer-to-consumer' engagements in which they share ideas, experiences, feelings and capabilities. Consumers are putting increasing pressure on *What, How, When, Where* they want products and services and *How Much* they are willing to pay for them. In other words, consumers increasingly are in a position to be involved in the activities previously thought of as internal to the organization.

Tapping into mass-consumer insights

But rather than perceiving these developments as a threat some companies are seeing it as a big opportunity by facilitating mass-consumer involvement and tapping into their insights. For such companies consumers have specialized competencies and skills that they are unable to match themselves or even understand. These companies are realizing the power of tapping into the insights and enthusiasm of thousands of their users. They do this by providing a creative and open communications environment where consumers can effectively apply and enhance their insights for the benefit of themselves, each other, and the company.

It seems that a new 'social exchange contract' has been constructed between some companies and their consumer communities. In this 'contract' companies offer consumers resources and a platform to create where consumers in return offer companies their insights, skills and time.

One of these companies is the Lego Group, who have been collaborating with consumer communities since 2005 as described in a recent MIT *Sloan Management Review* article.[26] The authors explain how Lego experienced a turbulent period from 1998 to 2004 characterized by escalating competitive pressures and financial losses. But in 2005 the then new CEO, Jorgen Vig Knudstrop, recognized that the benefits of co-creation with consumer communities were unmistakable. 'We think innovation will come from dialogue with the community', he told a convention in 2005.[27] In the same year Lego created the Ambassador Program to provide a fast and direct way for the company and its adult fans in particular to get into contact with one another. The program has provided considerable value to both the company and consumers. In their article the authors explain how for the Lego Group the program has offered exposure to new ideas, new technologies and new business partnerships. Management saw that not everything needed to be developed internally. Indeed the company has found ways to expand into new market areas without having to sustain long-term fixed costs. For the adult fans, collaborations have allowed them to influence Lego's business and strategic decisions resulting in the co-creation of not only new product lines for different target markets but also new distribution strategies. There were more than 150 known user groups with over 100,000 active adult collaborators worldwide.[28] All of this means that Lego can tap into the mass insights of a globally networked community as a critical input to their consumer strategy creation.

Not McDonaldizing 'co-creation'

We believe that co-creation with consumers can backfire when the underlying motivation is driven from the inside pursuing internal value rather than from the outside and in pursuit of true joint value. Realizing that we may have insightful consumers ready and eager to spend nights and weekends acting as extensions of our Research & Development or Strategy departments can't be our main driver. In other words, consumer co-creation is not enduring when we apply a McDonaldized approach. This is a term coined by academics where 'McDonald's restaurants turn customers into waiters and cleaning personnel'.[29] For instance, some academics argue that consumers are generally not paid for the insights, knowledge, and time that they contribute to the organization in this way. Instead, consumers typically end up paying a price-premium for the fruits of their own labour as the use value of the co-created product or service is often higher.[30]

Lego also came to the realization that a win-win needed to be ensured and that collaborations needed to be a rewarding experience for the users. According to the authors of the MIT Sloan article Lego tends to use intrinsic rewards by giving outside collaborators a combination of experience, access and free Lego products. However, collaborators who provide services and insights that are more like 'work' are apparently given a choice: 'they can receive free products or a more conventional stipend. In business partnerships between Lego and users ... various long-term, fee-based partnership agreements have been negotiated'.[31]

Bringing capabilities up to date

From the Lego example it becomes clear that in order to leverage the large pool of insights that consumer communities hold we need to ensure a win-win but also secure capabilities on two fronts. We need to secure the right people *and* the right technological capabilities. Firstly, we need to escape the company-centric image of the past. We can no longer be autonomous in developing consumer strategies. This means that from a cultural and behavioural perspective our people will need to be able and want to unlock insights collaboratively together with our consumers.

This intent then needs to be supported with the technological platforms for our people to capture the consumer insights and facilitate co-creation. We acknowledge that this is easier said than done. How many of us already struggle with keeping relevant our static Customer Relationship Management systems? But strategically creative and effective companies are putting *both* a consumer-centric culture and the right IT platforms to good use as the basis for co-creation and innovation.

Co-creating with additional stakeholders

The concept of co-discovering insights and co-creating strategies may not be 'limited' to the executive team, the board, the workforce, internal outsiders, customers, or mass-consumers as explored in this book. Depending on the industry and type of organization we may need perspectives and insights from additional stakeholders such as suppliers, shareholders, government, communities, investors, owners, unions, professional associations, or third-party advisors such as management consultants, independent strategy advisors, equity analysts, investment bankers, technology experts, economists, academics, and audit firms.

With some of the mentioned stakeholders we already may have enduring relationships. With others we may have to proactively develop our relation by investing more time and resources. The importance of these relationships has been stressed in a number of academic studies where relationship development can fruitfully be explained as a *social exchange process* in which two parties gradually and interactively learn about each other, build trust in each other and commit themselves to exchange with each other.[32]

We should not shy away from exchanging with some of our more 'difficult' stakeholders more often and more regularly. We perhaps should put more effort in developing these relationships further so that we can co-discover strategic opportunities that are of mutual benefit. By actively engaging with these stakeholders – who often tend to look at the world from a different paradigm – breakthrough moments can and do occur. These so-called *intersection moments* occur when parties and concepts from one field are brought into new and unfamiliar territory. Or, where established perspectives clash and come together with insights from other disciplines and cultures potentially resulting in an 'explosion' of new paradigms and innovation.[33]

We do acknowledge that developing relationships with various stakeholders is a time-demanding practice and that considerable managerial resources are involved. But there is a wide range of internal and external stakeholders that can or need to help us with their specific insights and with the co-creation of more distinctive and relevant strategies. There are so many moving pieces and so many variables impacting on our organizations today that we would make a mistake if we didn't call on stakeholders who are more insightfully diverse than we are.

5
Realizing Distinctive Strategies

Imagine top management having put a lot of effort in creating the organizational strategy and are now expecting the workforce to execute on the plan. Imagine also the subsequent scenario how employees become mechanically obedient, disillusioned and disconnected as poignantly described by Roger Martin in a *Harvard Business Review* article:

> Employees become blinded by the rigidness of the strategy execution model they have come to know, make high-level abstract choices and assume that everything else is simple implementation. They fail to recognize that the choices made at the top will beget a whole array of difficult choices down the line. If employees make sound choices and produce great results, senior management gets (and usually takes) credit for having put in place a great strategy. If, on the other hand, there are poor results (whether due to bad choices by management, by employees, or both), the conclusion will almost certainly be that there was flawed execution. ... This bind creates a sense of helplessness, rather than a sense of joint responsibility for success. Inevitably, employees decide simply to punch their time cards rather than reflect on how to make things work better for their corporation and its customers. It's a vicious circle. Feeling disconnected, employees elect not even to try to share customer data with senior managers. Senior managers then must work around their own organisation to get the data necessary to make decisions, typically by hiring outside consultants. Frontline employees find the resulting choices inexplicable and

unconvincing, because the data comes from outside the organisation. The employees feel even more disconnected from the company and more convinced, as Dilbert would say, that they are working for idiots. Senior management blames the frontline employees, frontline employees blame management, and eventually, everyone becomes belligerent. Management imposes executional rules and ways of operating that feel unilateral and arbitrary, and frontline workers act against the spirit of the strategy and withhold data that would aid in decision-making. In this cold, self-centered world, relationships between levels of the organisation do not develop or develop with mistrust. Reflection tends to be limited to what impact those in the rest of the system will have on an individual's ability to succeed; the person does not consider his own possible contribution to the problem. Finally, leadership tends to take too much responsibility for success by planning ever more complex strategies and ever more stringent implementation plans, while the middle- and lower-level managers see these efforts, feel helpless, and back off from taking responsibility.[1]

And the saga doesn't end here. It normally continues with the next step where leadership then turns to restructuring. In desperate efforts to still realize the original proposed change, they go right to structural measures because moving lines around the organizational chart seems the most obvious solution. What's more, the changes are visible and concrete.

We should avoid putting the cart before the horse. The first temptation always seems to be – implicitly or explicitly – to give an answer in terms of structures. In other words, to see the driving force for realizing the strategic change in the modification of organizational charts, in the re-arrangement of responsibilities, and in the amendment of rules and procedure.[2] Such steps generally reap some short-term efficiencies quickly. But in so doing address only the symptoms of dysfunction and not its root causes. Several years later organizations usually end up in the same place they started or worse.

Strategic dreams often turn into nightmares if companies start engaging in expensive and distracting restructurings. Given the costs and difficulties involved in finding structural ways to unlock

value Robert Kaplan and David Norton raise the question: 'Is structural change the right tool for the job?' They believe the answer is
usually no.[3]

The realization that organization and unlocking value do not conse-
quentially equate with structure is still not totally understood within
many of our organizations it seems. 'Organisations do not function
in accordance with their official definitions nor indeed with the rules
and procedures, so long and carefully weighed up'.[4] Of course structural change can and should be part of the path to improved execution but it is best to think of it as the capstone not the cornerstone of
any organizational strategic change.[5]

So, these are some of the inevitable costs of the mainstream strategy
execution approach. Unfortunately, the above-described scenario has
too often become a reality within our organizations. In this chapter,
we therefore examine the mainstream execution approach that does
not seem to be effective and explore alternative ways of realizing
strategic change. We use the terms 'strategy execution', 'strategy
implementation', 'acting on strategies', and 'realizing strategies'
interchangeably.

It is true that the best strategy is only as good as its implementation. Executing strategy enduringly is difficult. In a study asking
C-level executives to rank their most pressing business issues they
ranked how to more effectively execute strategy as their number one
challenge.[6] No wonder strategy execution keeps executives awake at
night. If various studies are to be believed, between 57 and 90 per cent
of companies stumble in the implementation phase and are unsuc-
cessful at executing their strategic initiatives.[7] In other words, the
created strategies are not implemented with the originally intended
results.

So, what are the obstacles to executing strategy? The surveyed
lists seem endless and relate to execution issues such as lack of time
and being too busy with operational challenges; the implementation taking considerably more time than originally allocated; major
problems surfacing that had not been identified beforehand; variables in the external environment having an adverse impact; lack
of clear and decisive leadership; leadership actions inconsistent with
strategy; competing activities and crises distracting attention from
the implementation; ineffective co-ordination and progress review of

implementation activities; lack of accountability or follow-through; unclear and unquantifiable tasks and activities; inability to measure impact; inability to make organizational strategy relevant across the various levels of the organization including front-liners; silos or units with competing agendas; resistance to change; and ultimately no critical mass of people who Can, Know and Want to realize the strategic change.[8]

Linking strategy creation and execution

But let's be frank. Most of the above reasons as to why execution fails are effects or outcomes. We believe that the underlying reason for failure has not so much to do with the execution of the strategy but with (disconnected) creation. Execution often fails because we haven't entirely gone through the comprehensive practice of strategy creation in the first place as described in Chapters 3 and 4. Before it even comes to execution, we may already have failed in co-creating *distinctive* strategies or a compelling story and subsequently gaining people's buy-in. By blaming the execution rather than critically looking at the original creation of the strategy, we tend to fool ourselves.

The popular explanation that 'a mediocre strategy well executed is better than a great strategy poorly executed' is totally misguided. It follows the common assumption that 'strategies most often fail because they aren't well executed'. But many strategies fail in the execution because indeed they *are* mediocre. How can executing a mediocre strategy ever be successful? Yet, we often hear executives proclaim that if they had to choose between a brilliant but poorly executed strategy and a mediocre but well executed strategy, they would choose the latter one.

The idea of a 'brilliant' strategy being poorly executed is evaluated in a *Harvard Business Review* article by Roger Martin. In this article, he questions:

> If a strategy produces poor results how can we argue that it is brilliant? It certainly is an odd definition of brilliance. A strategy's purpose is to generate positive results, and the strategy in question doesn't do that, yet it was brilliant? In what other field do we proclaim something to be brilliant that has failed miserably

in its only attempt? A 'brilliant' Broadway play that closes after one week? A 'brilliant' political campaign that results in the other candidate winning? If we think about it we must accept that the only strategy that can legitimately be called brilliant is one whose results are exemplary. A strategy that fails to produce a great outcome is simply a failure.[9]

A damaging distinction

Not only is the idea that a choice exists between a mediocre, well executed strategy and a brilliant, poorly executed strategy deeply flawed, so is the commonly held belief that strategy creation is distinct from strategy execution. An imaginary line exists in many of our organizations between strategy creation and execution. In other words, strategy is created by people above the line and executed by people below the line as illustrated in Figure 5.1.

The majority of managers believe that such an imaginary line exists between strategy creation and execution separating thinkers and doers.[10] According to this conventional belief, strategy is the purview of executives who – often aided by outside consultants – formulate it and then hand off its execution to the rest of the organization.[11]

But strategy is beyond executive monopolized creation as discussed in the previous chapter. We no longer can simply draw a line in our organizations above which executives merely

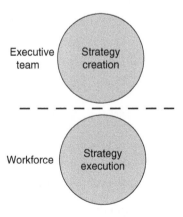

Figure 5.1   Imaginary line between strategy creation and execution

think of strategy and below which middle-managers merely *do*. Strategy is more than the executive team formulating it and then 'commanding' middle-level managers to go and make it happen. This approach assumes a logical and hierarchical distinction between strategy formulation and execution with execution delegated to a subordinate status as the responsibility of 'middle management'. In this accepted dogma execution is seen as more mundane and detailed compared to creating the grand vision and strategy for the future.[12]

There are two fundamental problems with drawing such a line between creation and execution. Firstly, it often creates an apathetic attitude amongst implementers. If strategy is created only by the executive team it really is not surprising when middle-managers and frontliners are less enthusiastic about executing something that they had no voice in creating.[13] It is easy to see how they can become mechanically obedient, disillusioned and disconnected.

The second problem with making a distinction or drawing a line between creation and execution is that today's strategy practices need a wider and deeper input from across (and outside) the organization as discussed in the previous chapter. We need to bring insights into both distinctive creation *and* enduring execution of our strategy. There are so many fast changing variables impacting on our organizations today necessitating a *continuous back-and-forth practice of strategic sensing, co-creation and execution*. So, we agree with several academics pointing out that we need to link strategy creation and execution as depicted in Figure 5.2.[14]

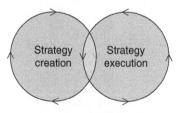

Executive team & Workforce

Figure 5.2 Linking strategy creation and execution
Source: Graeme Cocks, Melbourne Business School.

Middle managers don't just do

In our attempt to mobilize people and realize strategic change there is one critical group of employees that needs pointing out and that is *middle management*. Whether or not middle management is involved in the co-creation of the strategy, most organizations still rely mainly on middle managers for driving the implementation.

Yet, for the last quarter of the century such a panacea of delayering has taken place thereby stripping our organizations of their middle management. The term 'middle manager' in the West has even become synonymous with 'backwardness', 'stagnation' and 'resistance to change'.[15] Against this background middle managers have been bombarded over the years with various strategic change initiatives. These have been cascading from the top of our organizations demanding ever-increasing performance, competitiveness and efficiency through a constant stream of 'fads' and strategic initiatives.[16] All of this clearly has affected middle managers' behaviours and attitudes towards yet again having to implement the 'latest-flavour-of-the-month'. So, what are we expecting when yet again we launch the latest strategic change initiative within our organizations?

Removing or bypassing all middle managers simply won't work. Due to their structural positions the remaining middle managers are still key actors who can make or break any strategic change effort. Their organizational position allows them to obtain deep insights of both the external environment and the internal operations. Being usually closer to the markets and customers than executives, middle managers can bring divergent thinking into the shaping of the organizational strategy or help assess the viability of it. Middle managers can help evaluate the strategy in line with market trends and internal capabilities while also flagging risks or tradeoffs that might be required when implementing the strategy.[17] They can act as 'linking pins' and mediators between the organization's strategic and operational levels.[18] Moreover, middle managers have a strong influence in aligning and engaging the wider workforce.

So, middle managers are an integral part of a control system with our organizations and in a way hold the key to the ultimate enabling factor, the wider workforce. Gaining a critical mass of employees in support of strategic change will basically not happen without the full commitment of middle managers. Simply put middle managers are critical to realizing strategic change.

This reinforces our argument that we can't simply draw a line between strategy formulation by top management and execution by middle management. We need middle managers' insights and efforts in *both* strategy creation and execution. But research from around three decades ago has already informed us that middle managers will put very little effort into the implementation of a strategy if: [19]

1. They believe that they have a low probability of performing successfully in implementing that strategy; or
2. They believe that even if they do perform successfully individually, that performance has low probability of achieving the organizationally desired outcome; or
3. The organizationally desired outcome does not satisfy their individual goals -and hence needs

Additional research tells us that in order for middle managers to become proactively involved in the implementation, it is also essential for them to feel a sense of ownership of the strategy.[20] Again none of this is achieved in the conventional approach where strategy is formulated exclusively by the executive team and pushed down for middle managers to implement. How can such an approach enhance in any way middle managers' sense of ownership and belief in both individual and organizational abilities to successfully implement?

Countering implementation efforts

So, involving middle managers *throughout* the practice of strategic sensing, co-creation, and execution through sensemaking and dialogue is important. Limiting their involvement to just execution is simply naïve and can have unintended consequences. The unique strategic positions that middle managers hold within our organizations provides them with the opportunity to influence strategy activities positively, indifferently or even negatively.

The notion of 'counter effort' can be developed when middle managers feel that their self-interest is as stake. Middle managers who believe that their self-interest is being compromised by a strategic change initiative can not only redirect the strategy, delay its implementation or reduce the quality of implementation but can also even sabotage it.[21]

A study undertaken by researcher Sharon Turnbull reveals the varying commitment and behaviours of typologies of middle managers towards strategic change initiatives.[22] In her in-depth study many of the examined middle managers exhibited cynical, sceptical or indifferent behaviours towards a strategic change initiative. For instance, a number of middle managers manifested openly cynical behaviours. These 'open cynics' were often bitter, resentful, disruptive and disconcerting to others. They viewed the organizational change initiative as a manipulative and controlling tool of top management. Other middle managers were driven to just 'playing the game' due to their insecurity and distrust. These 'actors' 'preferred the route of *resigned behavioural compliance* whilst at work. They showed little emotional or moral involvement with the company, making it a policy to survive in what they perceived to be a ruthless political climate'.[23] There were many other middle managers exhibiting sceptical behaviours. These 'sceptics' were sceptical about the value of the strategic initiative and its chances of success together with the sincerity of top management. 'They tended to conform whenever they were exposed, preferring not to stand out from the crowd, but were openly sceptical amongst their peer group and often with their subordinates'. [24]

Influencing through sensegiving

The way counter efforts are displayed by middle managers and the organizational strategy is influenced can be subtle through political actions. The way middle managers politically influence their peers, subordinates, wider workforce and in some cases their superiors is through the practice of sense*giving*.

Sensemaking "has to do with the construction and reconstruction of meaning by middle managers as they attempt to develop a meaningful framework for understanding the nature of intended strategic change".[25] But sensegiving can be defined as 'the process of attempting to influence the sensemaking and meaning construction of others toward a preferred redefinition of organisational reality'.[26] In other words, sensegiving is much more than 'just' understanding the strategic change and has all to do with how middle managers *influence* different players in redefining the strategic change.

Scholars point out that sensegiving and organizational politics are interrelated as both concepts are about controlling and shaping others' meanings and perceptions of 'reality'. Academic Ole Hope explains that during strategic change there is fertile ground for alternative perceptions of reality but only one 'reality' will end up as the dominant and surviving 'reality'.[27] Therefore, the political struggle will be about the power of meaning. The power of meaning has to do with shaping others perceptions, cognitions and preferences which is about controlling what position will end up as the preferred direction. One can only imagine the sensegiving or influencing power that middle managers can possess over mobilizing or not their peers, subordinates and wider workforce.

In search of middle managers who Can-Know-Want

As several studies have shown middle managers play an important role in realizing strategic change. Their actions can be either convergent and hence support the strategic change initiatives or be divergent which means moving in a different direction compared with the strategic intent.

So, the point we are making is that for any strategic change initiative to be realized, we firstly need to gain a critical mass of middle managers who Can-Know-Want. Firstly, in terms of *Can*, middle managers need to believe that both at an individual and organizational level the capabilities exist for the strategic change to be implemented successfully. Secondly, in terms of *Know*, middle managers need to truly understand the strategy which is achieved only by being able to co-create it in the first place. Thirdly, in terms of *Want*, the strategic change needs to be congruent with middle managers' individual goals and self-interests. In the next chapters we will explore how this can be achieved not only with middle managers but the wider workforce.

Changing engines whilst flying the plane

Having highlighted the critical role of middle managers and the importance of linking strategy creation and execution into one continuous practice doesn't mean that execution itself is made easier. Newly created strategies per definition always relate to change. They are always on top of our day-to-day operational activities and challenges. So, realizing strategies feels like *having to change the engines whilst having to fly the plane at the same time*. Indeed there is nothing easy about realizing strategic change. It often becomes too hard and we quickly re-immerse ourselves into the day-to-day operational grind losing enthusiasm, focus and momentum. We retract to maintaining the status quo.

For the plane to keep on flying so to speak and strategic change to be realized we believe that ten (engine) components need to be practiced continuously as illustrated in Figure 5.3. The key components are all connected together to make the engine work and steer our organization towards realizing our strategy. The power of the model lies in its integrative approach as there are no primary or secondary components to the engine. All components are important. They are interrelated and *all* required to make strategic change happen.

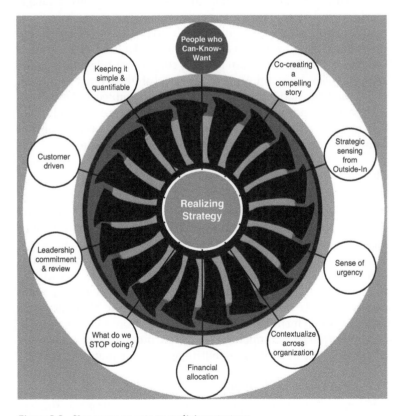

Figure 5.3 Key components to realizing strategy

The *strategic sensing* component

There is obviously no point to try and act on mediocre strategies. In our quest for distinctive strategies we need to go through the rigorous practice of continuous strategic sensing as described in Chapter 2. This means being aware of the limitations of our 'north view' or own inference. Therefore strategy sensing should not be from the Inside-Out. It should not be internally driven merely within our own paradigm based on conventional thinking. So, we have to stretch not only our strategic thinking but also our strategic seeing and feeling in our collective attempt to unlock deep insights. Being busy with the execution of our strategic plan doesn't mean that strategic sensing stops. This is a common pitfall for many organizations. Strategic sensing never stops because our environment *always* evolves. So, it requires an organizational agility and flexibility to continuously fine-tune or recreate strategic objectives that are about to or suddenly have become less relevant. We can't always stick to our originally created strategic plans and implement them regardless. Implementation plans can't be static documents and are undoubtedly destined to change. Customer and competitor responses, technological advances and resource allocation shifts can all impact on the timing and in some cases the scope of our original implementation plan.[28]

The *Can-Know-Want* component

We recognize that at the end of the day making any strategic change happen is truly a people's game. We may have succeeded in unlocking deep insights through seeing, feeling and thinking differently but to make any strategic change happen we need people who Can, Know and Want. All our execution efforts fail if we can't gain a critical mass of people who are able and willing to support the change, as discussed in Chapter 3. It is the ultimate and most comprehensive component because it deals with the strategic ability, strategic alignment and strategic engagement of our people. It is therefore too expansive to capture within this 'component paragraph' but is explored *throughout* all chapters of this book on mobilizing people for strategic change.

The *compelling story* component

For a critical mass of people to commit to executing the strategy enduringly they need to have contributed to a *compelling* story through continuous dialogue and sensemaking. A compelling story is made up of the seven 'simple' questions as explored in Chapter 3. For people to commit to enduring execution they need to personally identify with meaningful values, behaviours, purpose, vision, mission and not just a proposed strategic plan. Mediocre strategic plans don't mobilize people. So, we subsequently need to involve the workforce, the board, internal outsiders and co-create strategies with relevant stakeholders who are more insightfully diverse than we are as described in Chapter 4.

The *customer-driven* component

Trying to execute internally driven strategies is a recipe for disaster. Surely our starting point for creating and executing distinctive strategies has to be our customers. We don't merely view our customers as 'targets' and merely create internally driven strategies. Instead, our aim is to continuously build a true customer-centric practice where we leverage joint value through co-discovering and co-creating distinctive strategies. Business-to-Consumer organizations also need to tap into mass-consumer insights. For most of our organizations true customer- and consumer-driven strategies involves a cultural and behavioural shift. People need to both be able and want to unlock insights collaboratively from the Outside-In together with our customers or consumers as discussed in Chapter 4.

The *leadership commitment* component

Another key reason why many strategy implementations fail – astonishingly – is lack of enduring commitment of the CEO and executive team themselves. There is a danger of it all becoming too hard and many of the individual executive members retracting back to their own functional silos and business-as-usual. This is the point where we almost need to go-back-to-kindergarten so to speak. Where the CEO keeps the change momentum going by reviewing the progress of the organizational plan and by tracking the accountabilities not on an ad hoc basis but throughout the year. Such a review and tracking practice needs to happen monthly or even bi-weekly together with the strategic project owners and not bi-annually or quarterly. It is a basic and fundamental ongoing discipline that frankly is not practiced enough. It is also important for such progress review meetings not to fall back into operational discussions of day-to-day issues but

to keep the debate at a strategic level. Furthermore, short-term implementation wins need to be identified and celebrated.

The *urgency* component

The process of increasing urgency for the need for strategic change
is the most often overlooked component according to Professor John
Kotter.[29] The reason that a true sense of urgency is rare according to
Kotter is that it's not a natural state of affairs. It has to be created and
recreated. In organizations that have survived for a significant period
of time complacency is more likely the norm. Even in organisations
that are clearly experiencing serious problems business-as-usual can
survive. So, he warns that in a fast moving and changing world a sleepy
or steadfast contentment with the status quo can create disaster – literally. There is a constant need for an urgent focus on what is important.
What we are not promoting as Kotter points out is a false sense of
urgency that does have energized action but also has a frantic aspect
to it where people are driven by anxiety and fear. This dysfunctional
orientation prevents people from exploiting opportunities and exerting
extra-energies to realizing strategic change enduringly. Creating a sense
of urgency doesn't mean that we need to realize *all* of our strategic
objectives within the next 12 months. It is a natural tendency for most
of us to front-load strategic plans with short-term targets and actions
as the future is fraught with uncertainty. But healthy implementation
plans balance the short with the longer term and strive to portray the
full arc of the implementation process.[30] If our overall strategy for
instance is expected to be realized within three years then it should be
reflected within that span of time through a balance of both short and
longer term objectives and actions.

The *simple & quantifiable* component

For the execution to be successful our created strategies should be
simple, period! This doesn't mean that such strategies are easy to
create. People don't respond well to complex strategic plans however
neatly packaged as takeaways. Simple can be harder than complex
because you have to work hard to get your thinking clean to make it
simple as famously said by Steve Jobs.[31] Da Vinci saw simplicity as the
ultimate sophistication and Einstein argued that if we can't explain it
simply we don't understand it well enough. Complexity and compli-
cation creates uncertainty and inaction. So, there is a lot to be said for

keeping our strategic objectives and plans simple. Not only in terms of articulation but also in terms of number of objectives. How can we remember, communicate and realize 20-plus different objectives linked to a hundred or so actions within a 70-page strategic document full of analysis? The more so-called strategic priorities we have the more we will lose focus. More isn't necessarily better. We need to simplify but without dumbing down!

Besides keeping it simple we need to make sure our strategic objectives, actions and measurements are quantifiable. People simply can't execute mixed-up plans. Often we review strategic plans with objectives that have been mixed-up with actions or measurements. It is not uncommon, for instance, for organizations to have strategic 'objectives' such as 'we will increase our customer satisfaction from x to y per cent' or 'we will increase people engagement from x to y per cent within a period'. Both of these examples are not objectives but at best measurements. Objectives should be created in such a way that they encapsulate the underlying benefits or value propositions to our customers or people ultimately then resulting in increased satisfaction or engagement. Another example of a mixed-up 'objective' is 'we will understand our customers'. This can never be an objective but is at best an action that should lead to a wider objective that is of benefit to our customers. Our customers arguably couldn't care less if we are trying to understand them until this action leads to a wider benefit to them. That is what should be articulated through an objective.

The *STOP doing* component

Strategic objectives relate to change so they are always on top of our 'business-as-usual' activities. But this means that we can't just keep on going adding extra strategic activities to our day-to-day operational ones as time goes on. Yet this is a common mistake many of us make despite Peter Drucker warning that 'if you want something new you have to stop doing something old'.[32] It is just as important to decide what we will not do or stop doing as what we will start doing. So, we recommend 'Stop Doing' sessions in which we identify activities that aren't operational and mission critical. Such activities may once have been important and may have become the norm over the years but are less or not relevant anymore compared to our new direction and priorities. People need to be freed from such embedded activities so they can redirect their energies to executing on the new strategy.

The *financial allocation* component

Besides needing a critical mass of people who Can-Know-Want to realize the strategic change it seems axiomatic that financial resources for execution also must be allocated and reflected in our organizational budgets. Yet surprisingly many organizations fail to closely link the two activities. This is rightfully noted as a critical misstep in a *Journal of Business Strategy* article: 'Perhaps unintentionally, many firms prepare budgets first then turn to strategy development, a critical misstep. Strategy at the highest level describes a pattern of resource allocation; it delineates the playing field which the budget needs to accommodate, and not the converse'.[33]

So, the order is important. We don't want to restrict ourselves from an internal perspective to predetermined budgets without knowing the potential investment opportunities. For instance, if we truly managed to firstly unlock deep customer insights from the Outside-In resulting in the co-creation of *distinctive* strategies then surely being able to realize such strategies becomes the 'size-of-the-prize' worthy of adequate financial resourcing.

Unfortunately, in certain instances executive teams fail to allocate financial resources to the new strategic initiatives silently hoping against all odds that these strategies can be effectively executed through already existing operational budgets.

The *contextualizing* component

Execution efforts are not successful when we fail to contextualize our organizational strategy. For the organizational strategy to be realized it needs to be contextualized across the organization so it becomes relevant and meaningful to all employees at all levels. We may well have gone through the practice of co-creating a comprehensive story and plan at organizational level but often fail to then go through a similar process at divisional and departmental levels. Organizational strategies per definition are broad and therefore difficult to translate into concrete actions that employees can relate to at their level. So, groups of employees at divisional level need to 'cherry-pick' the strategic objectives from the organizational strategy that are of meaning to them within their own divisional context. Within their context they need to co-create their own compelling divisional story. It is important that the same practice and methodology is used at divisional level as was used at organizational level.

Is there, for instance, a *collective* understanding of where the division has come from in terms of what they have done well and what could have been done better? What are the division's key challenges, risks and weaknesses? What is the purpose of the division or how is the division adding value to whom with what kind of offering where? What does success look like for the division by when? Furthermore the divisional plan also needs to be (internal) customer centric and co-created from the Outside-In and in alignment with the organizational plan. This practice and methodology then needs to be repeated at departmental and arguably team levels. Throughout this practice across all levels we need thoughtful engagement through contextualized sensemaking and dialogue.

Realizing strategy through individual action

We often speak about three levels of strategy, whether it is organizational, divisional and departmental – or – corporate, business and functional. Contextualizing our plan across the three levels while a critical precondition is not enough. What contextualizing our strategy does is aligning people across the organization from a cognitive perspective. If done correctly it means that people at all levels *understand* how the organization's aspirations may translate into the divisional and departmental context.

But rarely do we acknowledge and translate it to the fourth level. This is the level of individual action – in which the grand (contextualized) strategies get translated into both practical and emotional implications from an individual employee's perspective. As academic Jeanne Liedtka points out 'without success at this final stage, the other three levels matter to no one other than the executives and consultants who create them. Platitudes and ROE targets are unlikely to be of much help at this stage'.[34]

So, strategies become significant only when leaders are able to help employees answer three 'simple' questions:

1. What does this mean to me in my role in this organization?
2. How can I contribute and make a difference?
3. Why should I care?

Within most of our organizations this fourth level or final stage is rarely addressed. But if a critical mass of employees can't answer these three questions at an individual level their workplace 'automatic pilot' will not be interrupted and proposed strategic change not realized. In the next chapter we explore how to build a critical mass of people who Can-Know-Want not only from organizational and group perspectives but critically from an individual employee perspective.

In closing this chapter it is clear to us that being able to realize distinctive strategies enduringly will emerge as the most critical source of competitive advantage in this century. Realizing organizational strategies through enduring execution has so far been a perennial challenge. Through our work we have been exposed to many executives who can describe their strategy. But ask them exactly how they plan to execute it and you typically get a very different response. It was around half-a-century ago that 'Peter Drucker wrote about the effective "execute-ive". His play on the word underscores the view that the key responsibility of being an executive is to execute to results – to go beyond being a thinker and a leader'.[35] Nothing has changed.

6
Overcoming Inertia

Imagine the following scenario. Imagine that in our quest for distinctive strategies we have gone through the rigorous practice of strategic sensing from the Outside-In as described in Chapter 2. Within our organization we have become aware of the limitations of our 'north view' or own inference. We understand that strategy creation should not be internally driven and developed merely within our own paradigm based on conventional thinking. So, we have continuously stretched not only our strategic thinking but also our strategic seeing and feeling in our collective attempt to unlock deep insights.

We also recognize that at the end of the day making any strategic change happen is truly a people's game. We may have succeeded in unlocking deep insights through seeing, feeling and thinking differently but to make any change happen we need to mobilize a critical mass of people who Can, Know and Want. So, we have facilitated opportunities for co-creating a compelling story through continuous dialogue and sensemaking of the seven 'simple' questions as explored in Chapter 3. We understand that people need to personally identify with true meaningful organizational values, behaviours, purpose, vision, mission and not just a proposed strategic plan.

We also realize the limitations of monopolized and periodic planning by the executive team. We subsequently have involved the workforce, the board and also internal outsiders. Importantly we have built a true customer-centric practice with the aim of leveraging joint value through co-discovering and co-creating distinctive strategies. We are also working on tapping into mass-consumer insights and co-creating strategies with relevant stakeholders who are more insightfully diverse than we are as described in Chapter 4.

When it now comes to realizing our strategy we understand the importance of linking strategy creation and execution into one continuous practice as discussed in Chapter 5. We have co-created a 'simple' and quantifiable organizational plan. We have allocated financial resources to our new strategic initiatives and have also identified what we will *not* do or stop doing. Furthermore, a sense of positive urgency has been created. The executive team is reviewing the progress bi-weekly and the CEO is tracking the accountabilities. Finally, we have contextualized our organizational plan across all divisional and departmental levels. *What possibly can still go wrong?*

We still fail to gain a critical mass of people who affectively will support the intended strategic change. Research indicates that around 60 per cent of a typical workforce are fence-sitters.[1] They represent the middle group of the bell curve as illustrated in Figure 3.1. They are passive, they are indifferent, and they are trapped by inertia. On the right side of the curve, accounting for around 20 per cent of the workforce, is the group made up of underground resisters, opponents, and emigrants. The left hand side of the curve, representing only 20 per cent of our typical workforce, welcome the strategic change and are willing to champion or at least support it. So why is this the case? Why is around 80 per cent of a typical workforce passive, indifferent or even resisting strategic change?

We are often asked a similar question: 'Why is resistance to strategic change and organizational inertia so pervasive and predictable despite our best efforts?'. First of all we believe that most organizations actually don't give it their best effort. They don't go through the rigorous practice of strategic sensing, co-creation of a compelling story, and contextualizing the strategic change across the organization as discussed above and throughout this book.

But even if we do, we rarely translate the strategic change to the final level – that of the individual employee. This is the level of the individual action in which the contextualized strategies get translated into emotional implications from an individual employee's perspective.

What contextualizing our strategy does is aligning people across the organization from a cognitive perspective as discussed in Chapter 5. If done correctly it means that people at all levels understand how the organization's aspirations may translate into the divisional and departmental context. Doing this correctly is quite an achievement in its own right. But it 'only' means that people *Know* the strategic change and it doesn't mean that they are affectively committed or *Want* from an individual perspective. Without success at this final stage contextualizing the other three levels matters to no one and intended strategic change merely remains a theoretical exercise.

When a majority of individual employees don't *Want* to make change happen we are paralysed by organizational inertia. In this chapter we look at overcoming such organizational inertia and realizing strategic change. But importantly we also explore inertia from a micro-sociological perspective or that from individual's perspective. We explore employees' individual willingness to invest themselves and expend discretionary effort to help realize strategic change and therefore the organization succeed. We use the terms people, employees, members, workforce, and staff loosely and interchangeably.

Organizational inertia – asleep at the switch

We define *organizational inertia* as the resistance of a critical mass of people to realizing organizational strategic change by withdrawing extra-energies. The concept of inertia is not new. 'There is always an inertia to be overcome in striking out a new line of conduct' as renowned novelist Thomas Hardy used to say.[2] But inertia is paralysing many of our organizations in today's volatile times when we can least tolerate it. New lines of conduct are required now more than ever. So, it is beneficial to look deeper into the concept of inertia, which is holding many of our organizations back.

To understand organizational inertia it is useful to think in terms of *insight* inertia and *action* inertia according to scholars.[3]

Insight inertia

Insight inertia occurs when we don't observe and interpret cues from our external and internal environments in time to determine and adjust organizational behaviour to meet market, customer, and internal demands for strategic change.[4] It is when we don't exert the extra-energies to unlock and discover deep insights through strategic sensing. It is when we are not able to make sense of the environment or to explain why certain changes happened at all.[5]

Insight inertia arises from an indifference to a continuous strategic sensing from the Outside-In. This lack of market and customer sensing is accentuated by failing to perceive critical threats, challenges, risks, and weaknesses in time. Insight inertia arises when we have withdrawn our energies and conveniently remain trapped within our 'north view' paradigm as discussed in Chapter 2. In other words, we keep holding on to mental models and practices that may have been successful in the past but have become less pertinent. Or, as scholars argue, we may all well be 'asleep at the switch'.

Action inertia

Being asleep at the switch indicates being immobile and indeed 'nothing happens until something moves', as stated by Albert Einstein.[6] We believe that action inertia can be described as movement or energetic activity. In our context, action inertia can therefore be described as the withdrawal of energies to realizing strategic change.

When it comes to being indifferent to unlocking deep insights it is perhaps not surprising that such an organizational attitude is then reflected in non-action or action inertia. Action inertia arises when our response to environmental activity is too slow or the information gathered is inadequate enough to generate corrective actions beneficial to the organization.[7] In other words, when we fail to unlock deep insights we subsequently fail to create strategies that are distinctive and indistinctive strategies are in turn impossible to action enduringly. Scholars therefore point out that insight inertia and action inertia compromise the learning and memory of our organizations.

Individual inertia – the elephant in the room

But for once let us start translating all of this at individual emotional level. This is the level of the individual action in which strategic change gets translated into emotional implications from a micro-sociological and psychological or an individual employee's perspective. This is the level and perspective where most of the strategic change literature stops. But we can't just continue to try and make strategic change happen merely from an organizational perspective.

Organizational inertia or a critical mass of people withdrawing energies can be overcome only by exploring the underlying drivers and consequences at employees' individual level. Micro-sociological and psychological aspects of organizational life that promote organizational inertia are a product of the foibles of human nature. We agree with some scholars that this critical aspect of organizational life is under recognized and frequently the undiscussable 'elephant in the room'.[8]

In this context, we explore micro-sociological and psychological theories and insights from individual employees' perspectives within the following sections of this chapter. We believe that understanding the withdrawal of energies and resistance of *individual* employees to realizing organizational change firstly is essential to then understanding and overcoming *organizational* inertia.

Withdrawing energies

> Your heart's not in it and you just come to work because you have to, and you just do your job, and that's it. I try not to take things to heart and give my self personally any more.[9]

The above verbatim is representative of the majority of our workforces where people don't appear committed to realizing strategic change and stop 'giving themselves personally'. Psychologist William Kahn describes such behaviours by which individual employees start leaving out their personal selves:

> The simultaneous withdrawal and defence of a person's preferred self in behaviours that promote a lack of connections, physical, cognitive, and emotional absence, and passive, incomplete role performances. To withdraw preferred dimensions is to remove personal, internal energies from labours.[10]

In other words, individual employees actually remove or withdraw their physical, cognitive, and emotional energies from realizing the strategic change.

At the most basic level an example of *physical withdrawal* could be for instance not showing up or coming up with excuses for not attending strategy meetings. Or, scheduling and prioritizing operational engagements over and above any strategic change related encounters.

An example of *cognitive withdrawal* could be not sharing relevant skills, knowledge and insights that could benefit the strategy creation or execution. Or, people could cognitively withdraw by simply not asking for extra resources required to make the strategic change happen. This would then allow them the excuse of 'Oh but we were understaffed' 'justifying' underperformance or not delivering.

The verbatim used at the beginning of this section is an example of *emotional withdrawal*. It relates to people distancing themselves from any involvement with realizing the strategic change. They don't exert any extra-energies for the betterment of the organization and at best just do their day-to-day job. They don't make any strategic contribution or take any initiative and are merely getting through the day 'on automatic pilot'.

Physically uninvolved, cognitively unvigilant, and emotionally disconnected

The consequences should be no surprise to anybody. How can we expect our strategies to be realized when the majority of our workforces have become 'physically uninvolved in tasks, cognitively unvigilant, and emotionally disconnected from others in ways that hide what they think and feel, their creativity, their beliefs and values, and their personal connections to others'?[11]

But this is exactly what is happening in many of our organizations and the core reason as to why so many strategies fail, we believe. Organizations are failing to gain a critical mass of individual employees who are affectively committed to not just their jobs but to making organizational change happen. For reasons that will be explored in this chapter, too many people are not exerting extra-energies for the betterment of the wider organization but instead are withdrawing them to merely fulfilling their specific job requirements as illustrated in Figure 6.1. They aren't willing to invest themselves and expend discretionary effort to help the organization realize strategic change.

If anything they perform strategic tasks at some distance from their preferred selves which remain split off and hidden as described by William Kahn. The consequences of employees being physically uninvolved, cognitively unvigilant, and emotionally disconnected can be seen at *both* individual and organizational levels. Based on our

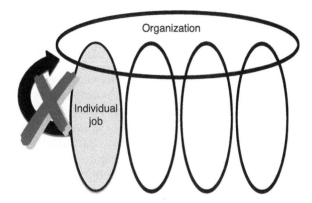

Figure 6.1 Withdrawing extra-energies that support the wider organization

own empirical research such individual behaviours have a significant impact on performance, productivity, innovation, organization citizenship behaviour, morale, culture, customer centricity, and retention of high performing staff.[12]

For instance, people who withdraw their energies perform strategy roles as external scripts rather than internally interpret those roles. At best they act as lip servers rather than champions and innovators. In other words, they don't exert energies to seeing, feeling and thinking differently about novel ways for improving the organization. They don't go out of their way to unlock deep insights and help co-create distinctive strategies.

We also found that withdrawing extra-energies impacts on organizational citizenship behaviour (OCB). These are behaviours of benefit to the wider organization that go beyond the basic requirements of the job and are to a large extent discretionary.[13] In our context, such behaviours are critical to facilitating organizational strategic change. But our findings suggest that when people withdraw themselves OCB diminishes. For instance, we observed lack of colleagues voluntarily helping each other with trying to realize change. Instead people would hide behind their role with attitudes like 'If it's not within my area I'm not going to help you'. We observed majority of workforces not demonstrating performance over and above what was expected. People would 'undermine' the organization in this way because they would do only the bare minimum in relation to their job and not take any initiatives that would benefit the organization. We noticed such an attitude easily spreading over to colleagues with everybody thinking 'if they're not doing that task, why should I?'[14]

Importantly, we observed that people who withdraw their energies don't attempt to see, feel and think form a customer perspective in order to unlock deep insights and help co-create distinctive strategies. They don't look from the Outside-In but retract to their internally driven perspective. Such a passive internal attitude manifests itself through a *can't-do* customer service culture or *computer-says-no* culture as satirically portrayed in the Little Britain television series. Equally, colleagues from other departments aren't viewed and treated as 'internal customers'. People just sit in their 'safe zone' not wanting to venture out and be proactive. In other words, people literally sit in their little cocoons and just hope that the phone doesn't ring and nobody requests anything. If requests are made then 'they hit the ceiling' with the reasons why things can't be done.

It is not surprising that the described damaging consequences have an ultimate impact on morale at both an individual and organizational level. At the individual level, it negatively impacts the state of psychological wellbeing based on a diminished sense of confidence, usefulness and purpose. At the organizational level, it negatively impacts the spirit of the organization that makes employees wanting the strategic change to be realized and the organization to succeed.[15] Without such an *esprit de corps* among the majority of the workforce strategic change simply will not be realized.

Finally, our research indicates that in an environment where the majority of the workforce withdraws their energies loss of talent and high performers are inevitable. We observed that two-out-of-three 'high potentials' felt that such a disengaged environment would make them leave as soon as an opportunity arose. We noticed that in such environments high-performers leave more often than poor performers. With high performers leaving there is obviously a consequential loss of experience, insights, expertise, and relationships that people have generated during their time of employment. This is a disengaging consequence for remaining staff who are left having to pick up the voids leaving them to 'reinvent the wheel' and also having to spend time training any replacement staff.

Why do individual employees withdraw energies?

Having described the demobilizing consequences of employees withdrawing energies raises an important question. Why wouldn't individual employees be willing to expand discretionary effort to realize strategic change and help the organization succeed? The emphasis of our discussion here is on the 'willing' or 'wanting'.

Surely at the most basic level employees need to feel that they *Can* or are proficient to fulfil the strategic change requirements of the organization. Obviously, employees need to have the right competencies and skills to make the change happen; otherwise they need to be offered relevant training and development.

Secondly and as discussed previously employees need to *Know* and cognitively understand the organizational change requirements. In other words, the organizational strategy needs to be contextualized and employees need to be strategically aligned. But assuming that we have gone through these practice as described throughout this book the question remains, 'why individual employees wouldn't *Want* to exert extra-energies supporting the organizational strategic change?' We seem to be left with a knowing-wanting gap. Research from individual employees' perspectives points to three fundamental reasons as to why such a gap exists:[16]

1. Not feeling valued and understood
2. Psychological contract violation
3. No idiosyncratic value proposition for realizing change

It is notable that the first two reasons as to why individual employees wouldn't want to exert extra-energies to realizing strategies have to do with issues related to their normal job environment and not necessarily with intended organizational change.

1. You don't make me feel valued and understood

Why would I go into fifth gear to help realize organizational change on top of my operational challenges when I don't even feel valued and understood in my day-to-day job? This is a disturbing but common sentiment among the majority of employees according to our research.[17] The biggest driver from individual employees' perspectives for *not* exerting extra-energies is not feeling valued and understood predominately by their line manager or supervisor.

A perturbing observation from our research is that the majority of employees feel that their direct line manager has a negative influence on their job engagement which also results in the withdrawal of energies to making organizational change happen. More specifically, the majority of employees don't feel that there is enough two-way communication, regular and informal feedback, involvement in decision-making, understanding of workload, empowerment, acknowledgement of work-life balance, and the most important influencing factor as generically perceived by employees – recognition.

Not feeling recognized by the direct line manager or supervisor for contributions is perceived to be the single most important driver from an employee's perspective for not exerting extra-energies and help realize the organizational strategy.

We find such findings incredibly disappointing. Realizing strategic change is ultimately a people game. It is about the ability of leaders and managers to take people on a journey collectively towards a preferred direction in an aligned and engaged manner. Our people are the ultimate enabling factor of making any distinctive strategy happen. So, people-managers within our organizations occupy critically strategic positions. Yet too often we observe that such managers are recruited and promoted into these positions mainly on specific job skills, competencies, and expertise. Sure, they may have many years of related vocational experiences but many of them we found aren't necessarily good people managers. Based on specific expertise and experiences they are then put in charge over teams, departments, divisions, or organizations but without being able to make their troops feel valued and understood nor recognized.

Moreover in many cases people managers renege on certain promises made to individual employees. From an employee's perspective such as breach or violation of promises can be a major driver for withdrawing energies and not affectively commit to helping realize the organizational strategy.

2. You've violated our psychological contract!

The second key reason why individual employees wouldn't want to exert extra-energies to realizing the organizational strategy directly relates to psychological contract violation.[18] This is an unfortunate phenomenon that is common with as many of two-thirds of employees saying their employer patently violated their psychological contract.[19] Some academics would argue this figure to be even higher.[20] So, what is the psychological contract?

The concept of the psychological contract is not new and is commonly traced back to the early work of Chris Argyris.[21] In the early 1960s, he recognized the impact of line managers or supervisors on employee behaviour and productivity through their leadership styles and a 'psychological work contract'.

The psychological contract can be defined as the perceptions of both the individual and the organization of the reciprocal promises and obligations implied in the employment relationship.[22] These promises and obligations represent a set of beliefs regarding the relationship between the individual and the organization. These beliefs are based on perceptions and therefore exist in the eye of the beholder or in the minds of the parties.[23]

Whilst scholars have been exploring the psychological contract for more than half-a-century, we don't feel the concept is widely understood among practitioners. Such a lack of understanding presents a problem when it comes to making strategic change happen. Our research tells us that the extent to which a psychological contract is honoured or violated influences in how far an employee will either exert or withdraw energies in relation to not only the job but importantly to helping realize strategic change.[24] In other words, the psychological contract can influence the investment of our energies and emotions to not only our work but also to the wider organization. So, it makes sense to delve a bit deeper into this concept.

Fairness and trust are closely implicated with the psychological contract. Employees weigh up in how far promises and obligations have been met and whether they are fair. In other words, whether the psychological contract has been delivered or not. If individual employees perceive that the deal is being delivered then there are positive attitudinal and behavioural outcomes. From an organizational perspective such outcomes relate to increased organizational commitment and organizational citizenship behaviours.[25] These are clearly desirable attitudes and behaviours needed for realizing organizational change.

But here it comes. When individual employees feel that the organization breaks perceived promises and obligations then a variety of negative attitudinal and behavioural outcomes can be expected impacting on any organizational change effort. Prior to exploring such outcomes we single out different levels of severity and consequences. We can distinguish between psychological contract *breach*, which is quite common but mostly inconsequential, and *violation*, which is far more emotive with more serious behavioural consequences. It is more intense and therefore more personalized.

Psychological contract violation results in strong affective responses to more extreme breaches of contract such as feelings of injustice, betrayal, and deeper psychological distress whereby the victim experiences anger, resentment, a sense of wrongful harm.[26] It can also evoke other extreme emotions such as disillusion, bitterness, bereavement, indignation, hate, and outrage. Thus psychological contract violation is a deep emotional state that we should try to understand given that the majority of workforces have experienced it and given the considerable consequences on our ability to realize strategic change. We simply can't expect to mobilize people when the majority of them are feeling disillusioned, bitter or resentful.

So, an important question becomes, *what causes psychological contract violation?* It can occur when there is perceived outcome discrepancy or reneging on promises. This can relate to perceived broken promises around financial rewards, career development, training and development, and benefits or unmet expectations in relation to organizational values and behaviours. It can occur when an employee feels, for instance, that a pay raise or promotion was promised to him or her but not given. But it also can occur when an employee perceives that certain financial rewards or promotions, for example, are unfairly distributed to other employees. Or, it can relate to certain promises made during recruitment around the work itself or advancement opportunities which then aren't perceived to be honoured once appointed. Or, it can occur when employees believe that their deal included a degree of job security.[27] The extent to which the organization is then perceived to handle redundancies fairly and displays reciprocal commitments to both leaving and 'surviving' employees can equally be a factor.[28]

The problem with psychological contract violation is that it hurts both parties. Sure, employees suffer directly and daily but we should realize that the organization suffers indirectly but nevertheless severely as a consequence. For decades researchers have highlighted the wide array of negative attitudinal and behavioural outcomes of contract violation. They have warned us of subsequent organizational ineffectiveness and underperformance. Yet it seems to have fallen on deaf ears for many organizational leaders and people managers. Let's consider the negative *attitudinal* outcomes of contract violation. Researchers point out lower levels of job satisfaction, of organizational commitment, of trust in the organization, and to higher levels of cynicism and neglect of job duties. Negative *behavioural* outcomes relate to withdrawal behaviours resulting in lower organizational citizenship, lower extra effort, increased absenteeism, and increased intention to quit.[29]

As if such negative outcomes are not enough to immobilize a workforce our own empirical research[30] tells us that psychological contract violation is a key driver for individual employees to not only *withdraw* their energies when it comes to supporting organizational change but in several cases *redirect* their energies towards retaliatory behaviour or anti-social behaviour or misbehaviour.[31]

The dark behavioural consequences

Within our organizations people give and people get. In other words, they are in what scholars call a *social exchange relationship*. Following this school of thought people give their energies physically, cognitively, and emotionally in return for financial rewards, benefits, development, recognition and so on. Where the equation is balanced then all is well but where it is not, people are motivated to re-establish it. This 're-establishment' can take the form of withdrawal of energies with the discussed attitudinal and behavioural outcomes.

But it is not uncommon, we found, for people who feel undervalued, frustrated, betrayed or whose psychological contracts have been violated to *right a wrong*. In this case, people don't just withdraw their energies but they redirect them through more extreme organizational misbehaviour or counterproductive behaviours at work.

Organizational misbehaviour or anything you do at work that you are not supposed includes the widest range of behaviour from failure to work very hard or conscientiously, through not working at all, deliberate output restriction, practical joking, pilferage, sabotage, or sexual misconduct according to scholars.[32]

A similar term *counterproductive behaviours at work* (CWB) is often used synonymously with anti-social, deviant, dysfunctional, retaliative and unethical behaviour at work.[33] It can be described as voluntary behaviour of organizational members that violates significant organizational norms and in doing so threatens the well-being of the organization and its members.[34] Organizational norms can be violated through eleven groups of counterproductive behaviours at work: misuse of information, misuse of time and resources, unsafe behaviour, poor attendance, poor quality work, alcohol use, drug use, inappropriate verbal actions, inappropriate physical actions, theft and related behaviour, and destruction of property.[35]

Based on our own empirical research we found that psychological contract violation was a perceived driver for people to engage in counterproductive behaviours exemplified through bullying, fraud, lying, breaches of confidentiality, and non-compliance of organizational rules and processes.[36]

Again, all of these are misbehaviours attributing to cultures clearly not conducive to mobilizing people for strategic organizational change. But it raises the question as to *how* people are being managed by line managers and supervisors for such counterproductive behaviours to be displayed in our organizations.

3. Where's my idiosyncratic change proposition?

We rarely acknowledge and translate organizational strategic change to the 'fourth' level of individual action in which our organizational, divisional, and departmental strategies get translated into both practical and emotional implications from an individual employee's perspective. As we pointed out in the previous chapter, without success at this final stage, the other three levels matter to no one other than the executives and consultants who create them.

So, strategies become significant only when leaders are able to help individual employees answer 'simple' questions such as 'How will this change affect me?' 'How can I contribute and make a difference?' and 'Why should I care?'

We found that within most organizations this fourth level or final stage is rarely addressed. But if a critical mass of employees can't answer these questions at an individual level they most likely will withdraw their energies and resist the intended organizational strategic change. Why?

Renowned scholars such as Manfred Kets de Vries note that psychological resistance to change arises from a desire to avoid the emotional pain associated with confronting the state of one's self. In other words, we will try to maintain a familiar equilibrium regardless of how dysfunctional, self-defeating and self destructive that equilibrium may be.[37] We tend to develop a defensive resistance to knowing what will happen if we feel that our inner conflicts and defences are challenged by the intended change. Destabilizing this balance threatens the loss of our carefully created and balanced psychological defences and self-images.

So, by acknowledging that change is needed a distressing personal disorientation emerges that may be described as peering into the empty void of the self. For many of us it is simply too painful to call into question and having to change our well established sense of self or *false self* as academics coin it.[38] In other words we all have a 'north view' of our own self and this false self is a life-long, psychologically defensive construct that is being challenged by intended change. Asking people to approach their work differently requires not just cognitive shifts but also places emotional demands on their feelings of self-competence, of self-confidence, and of self-esteem at work.[39]

Our point is that such apprehensions or resistance at the individual level must be confronted, clarified, and interpreted through sense-making and dialogue. There is a critical role to be played here for line managers or supervisors of individual employees. They will need to help their direct reports answer in an idiosyncratic manner how the change affects them personally, what they can do individually to contribute, and why they should care. This can be achieved only in an open, inclusive, collaborative, listening and respectful environment. It sounds obvious but we simply don't see this practiced at individual level enough in many organizations.

What are the key drivers for exerting extra-energies?

We all know what organizations want; they want an engaged and committed workforce willing to exert extra-energies. Of course that's what employers want because an engaged and committed workforce equals higher performance and higher productivity.[40] But that's an ultimate effect or outcome. The real question becomes: what is it that employees want? Or, in other words what are the generic and underlying drivers – very much from individual employees' perspectives – that will result in the exertion of extra-energies not 'just' within their jobs but also for the betterment of the wider organization?

Potential drivers for exerting extra-energies

When asking employees what the key drivers are for them to exert (or withdraw) extra-energies we found that around sixty drivers can be identified. These sixty drivers can be grouped into six categories in relation to the organizational environment, the job environment, financial rewards, benefits, training and development, and the state of the psychological contract as illustrated in Figure 6.2.[41]

What do those sixty drivers as perceived by individual employees tell us? First of all, there seems to be a surprisingly *large* number of different and multifaceted drivers. Secondly, we found that the perceived importance of each of these drivers differs among many individual employees or even groups of employees. So, being a people

Organizational environment	Job environment
• Values, culture, reputation, ethics, leadership, vision, strategy, communication, human resources practices, equality of opportunities practices, health and safety practices, social responsibility practices, bureaucracy, and general policies and procedures	• Job compatibility, job characteristics, line-manager relations, co-worker relations, job variety, control, autonomy, work-life balance, communication, decision making, health and well-being, performance and appraisal, fair treatment, and physical job environment
Financial rewards	**Benefits**
• Salary, financial incentives, bonus, paid overtime	• Pension contribution, health insurance, annual leave, sick leave, maternity leave, parental leave, on-site child care or child care subsidy, flexible working, company vehicle, laptop, mobile phone, home internet connection, parking, health and wellness programs, casual dress code, office location, life insurance
Training and Development	**Psychological contract**
• Training, development, career advancement, job sharing, job rotation, mentoring, coaching, and learning opportunities.	• Reciprocal promises and obligations, delivery of the deal, contract breach and violation, fairness and trust

Figure 6.2 Potential drivers for exerting (or withdrawing) extra-energies

manager is quite complex. Trying to understand which of the drivers are of most importance to each of your direct reports is difficult and requires insights. Incidentally, we are not always convinced that the majority of people managers are investing enough time and effort into unlocking such insights and discovering the key drivers among their people.

What is it that employees really want?

There can be a very simple answer to this question. The most basic motivator is the same for all of us – to feel good about ourselves and what we are doing.[42] We all want to do things worth doing, we want to achieve things and feel good about ourselves. When we feel good it is fundamentally because we have a sense of psychological well-being.[43] It is the extent to which we experience a positive sense of purpose at work.

It should go without saying that of all sixty drivers *health and well-being* has to be the most important driver. Positive psychological well-being at work means that people are inspired, alert, excited, enthusiastic, determined, happy, and contented.[44] They are inspired, determined and enthusiastic to not only doing their job but to exerting extra-energies for the organization. Psychological well-being is an affective state and fundamental in mobilizing people for strategic change.

Building an affectively committed workforce involves using leadership behaviours and organizational practices that enhance and sustain psychological well-being and importantly are not damaging to psychological well-being. This sounds obvious but the psychological health of employees in many of our organizations is poor.

Thus at the most basic level, individual employees should experience positive psychological well-being. This should include psychological safety or feeling able to show and employ one's self without fear of negative consequences to self-image and status.[45] Assuming individual employees have a positive sense of psychological well-being then:

> What is the most critical driver for exerting extra-energies as generically perceived by employees?

The 'simple' answer is RECOGNITION.[46]

The longing for recognition

It seems obvious doesn't it? How can we expect people to go into fifth gear and realize the organizational strategy *without* recognizing their contributions? But the majority of people in our organizations don't feel recognized.[47] So what's happening?

For once most academics don't seem to have the answers either. There barely seems any academic research undertaken into the concept of employee recognition. In stark contrast the practice literature is inundated with self-help-style books on the topic. But these 'popular' books aimed at practitioners seem to focus on how to save money while obtaining better business results through typical reward programs including awards, events, perks, and privileges. In our context, we are not talking about such rewards. Let's be clear – neither are we talking about giving away two cinema tickets or reserving a parking lot for our 'employee of the month'.

Distinguishing between recognition and reward

Most of us talk about 'reward and recognition' interchangeably but employees do perceive them very differently. Linking reward and recognition in this way is unfortunate and diminishes the critical role of recognition. Our own research tells us that reward is not perceived as the most critical driver for exerting extra-energies but recognition is. So, what is the distinction?

Reward is a formal, impartial, and equitable exchange. A material or financial expression of appreciation that is conditional on results.[48] *Recognition* is constructive and genuine feedback based on acknowledging people and their contributions. Among the few academics who comprehensively have analysed employee recognition are Brun and Dugas from Laval University in Canada who define the concept as:

> Recognition is first and foremost a constructive response; it is also a judgment made about a person's contribution, reflecting not just work performance but also personal dedication and engagement. Lastly, recognition is engaged in on a regular or ad hoc basis, and expressed formally or informally, individually or collectively, privately or publicly, and monetarily or non-monetarily.[49]

Recognizing recognition: the why, what, how, who, and when

We can't reiterate enough the critical role that recognition plays when it comes to employees wanting to exert extra-energies not only within their current roles but particularly to supporting any organizational change. We suspect that many people-managers may have a false-sense of understanding this concept. To gain a deeper insight we explore seven key questions related to recognition from an individual employee's perspective.

1. Why should I be recognized?
2. Do I feel recognized?
3. What should I be recognized for?
4. Who should recognize me?
5. How should I be recognized?
6. When should I be recognized?
7. What happens if I am not recognized?

The above seven questions will be explored vis-à-vis our own research findings, the relevant literatures on recognition, and Brun and Dugas' comprehensive analysis of employee recognition as published in *The International Journal of Human Resource Management*.[50]

1. Why should I be recognized?

A philosophical reason given by academics is that people should be recognized because failing to show gratitude to those who deserve it offends against the norms of society. They go on to say the unrecognized person in the workplace soon becomes dispirited.[51]

Regardless of status and job type every employee feels a need to be recognized by superiors, co-workers, and customers; everyone wants to be fully appreciated and acknowledged as individuals and workers.[52]

Our own research confirms that nearly all employees want their contributions to be recognized because it makes them feel 'special' or at least 'more than a number'. Employees want to feel valued for personally contributing value or for the worth that they provide to the organization. In some cases they want to be recognized of value as equal or sometimes even greater value 'than what some of the other people around the place are doing'. Basically employees want their organizations and line managers to recognize that they're an integral player.

From an academic perspective, Brun and Dugas identify four arguments for employee recognition: ethical, humanistic or existential, psychodynamic, and behavioural. The *ethical* discourse promotes the idea that recognition is about human dignity and social justice. Not just about organizational performance. Closely related to the ethical argument is the *humanistic or existential* one where recognition is immediately granted to everyone based on the principle of equality among people by virtue of their common humanity. The *psychodynamic* argument is concerned with people's subjective experiences in the workplace and their attempt to maintain a psychological balance in disconcerting working conditions. In maintaining balance between suffering and pleasure at work, recognition is a pleasure or 'reward' expected by employees. The *behavioural* discourse argues that human behaviour is controlled by its consequences within an effort-reward model; thus recognition becomes a method for positively reinforcing actions and behaviours considered desirable by the organization.

It is surprising that so many employees perceive a lack of recognition.[53] If the ethical, humanistic, existential, psychodynamic or behavioural reasons are not persuasive enough, there always is the *financial business case* reason. We find it extraordinary why so many employees perceive a lack of recognition because it costs the organization nothing. Or, as some scholars state – 'it is all the more extraordinary in this materialistic world because it costs nothing to ring up or go the office and say thank you. Recognition and praise are cheap and done effectively and judiciously can be particularly motivating'.[54] Not only does it cost the company nothing the return on this 'zero cost investment' makes employees exert extra-energies within and outside their current tasks.

2. Do I feel recognized?

The simple answer is that the majority of employees in our organizations don't feel recognized.[55] It is disheartening and clearly not the ideal starting point for asking people to start exerting extra-energies and make intended organizational change happen.

Whilst the majority of our workforces don't feel recognized individual employees respond in various ways to this question. Many even respond by saying that it has never happened to them. Or, they answer the question indirectly 'on behalf of' their peers by saying 'people are pulling out a lot of stops and not getting patted on the back as often as they should be'. Others react guarded about being recognized as they link being recognized to ending up with raised targets and increased workloads. Sentiments like 'if they do recognise that you're overdoing your job they will start increasing your workload further' are not uncommon.

Additional sentiments are unlocked by asking employees why they think they do not receive recognition. Some blame themselves due to just getting on with the job and not being in everybody's face. Other employees feel they aren't being recognized simply because they work in a support function which is not being perceived as 'adding value' by others in the organization. Many employees contribute not being recognized to organizational matrix structures with multiple reporting lines and therefore not getting noticed. Many of today's roles are indeed 'self-managed' and people are resourced for a number of different line-managers. As a result no one actually understands the workloads of individuals with employees 'getting hammered by a lot of different people'.

So, overall employees don't feel recognized at all. Our findings are consistent with most employee-opinion surveys reporting that employees across all levels feel unappreciated and not recognized whether they are middle management, floor staff, or senior employees.[56]

Senior employees not receiving recognition themselves was the main finding of a survey amongst members of the International Public Management Association for Human Resources in the United States and Canada. When senior managers do not receive recognition themselves, it perhaps makes it hard to know expectations or how to give it? [57] But it is amazing to see what happens when senior managers are recognized themselves. We recall running a workshop with a group of senior general managers from a large bank. At one point we asked the executives, 'When was the last time you received recognition for your efforts?' After a period of silence, one of the executives spoke up. He recounted working back one night when, at about 8 o'clock, the bank's chief executive who was leaving for the night stepped into the executive's office, put his hand on his shoulder and said 'You shouldn't be working this late but I really appreciate the time and effort you're putting into the job – thank

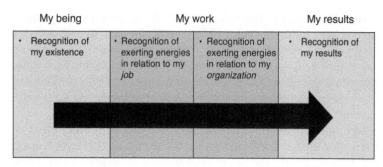

Figure 6.3 Forms of employee recognition
Source: Adapted from the work by Brun and Dugas.[58]

you'. It was an important moment for the executive who got teary as he recalled the encounter.

3. *What should I be recognized for?*

Employees can be recognized for their being, for their work, and for their results as illustrated in Figure 6.3.

My Being

Understanding and appreciating an employee's being is *existential recognition* and is purely based on the underlying belief that people should be recognized for their being or their unique, distinctive character, identity and expertise. This form of recognition is found in everyday interaction and is expressed for no other reason than individuals being human.[59]

At first we were somewhat reserved about such a 'hippy' statement having to recognize people just for their 'being'. But our own research findings are causing us to rethink our preconception. We found that around a quarter of employees don't feel recognized for their 'existence'. Such sentiments are based on their line managers for instance: 'not even saying "good morning"...what does it cost saying "good morning"' or 'looking down at you, you're just a worker' or executives 'not remembering my name even though we used to work together'. So, when we fail to acknowledge employees at the most basic level we should not be surprised when people withdraw their energies from making organizational change happen.

It should not take a lot to acknowledge people's being. But to really understand, appreciate, and recognize an employee's being, a line manager has to take interest. Without taking such an individual interest we simply don't understand the key drivers that motivate people. Good people-managers are truly interested and know what the key motivating drivers are for each of their direct reports across the six categories illustrated in Figure 6.2.

My Work
First and foremost what employees really long for is being recognized for their efforts in relation to their jobs. Clearly if an employee has worked extra it is nice to know people are watching and acknowledging. When employees 'go-into-fifth-gear' and exert extra-energies within their job roles – independent of results by the way – it is critical that such effort and dedication are recognized. This type of recognition relates to the level of participation, commitment and contribution shown by an employee in their job. If such job dedication is not being recognized employees will go 'back-into-third-gear' and will withdraw energies not only from their job but also from any intended organizational change effort.

Once employees feel that their efforts in relation to their jobs are being recognized they also may exert energies supporting the organizational strategic change. But if their effort at organizational level is not being recognized they then will quickly withdraw their extra-energies supporting the organizational change. In other words, most employees won't put any extra effort in making organizational change happen if their job dedication is not firstly recognized.

My Results
Recognition of results bears directly on the end product. It is a judgment and a mark of gratitude based on the efficiency, usefulness, and quality of work performed by an employee. It also involves an evaluation of an employee's performance and productivity and is expressed only when the task has been completed according to Brun and Dugas. We found that employees sometimes may fall short of expected results despite their best efforts. There often are many 'uncontrollable' variables impacting on the ability of employees to achieve certain predetermined results. When those results are not realized employees tend to miss out on any acknowledgment despite their best efforts.

So, in certain cases 'it would be proper nonetheless to recognise the quality and intensity of the energy brought to the task'.[60] In other words, recognizing the 'dedication to work' rather than just the 'results'. Such as practice could also be an opportunity to highlight the contribution for instance of 'behind-the-scenes' or back office workers.

4.   *Who should recognize me?*

From employees' perspective there are a variety of constituents who could express recognition. They can be employees' direct line manager or supervisor, their peers or team members, others in the organization, executive leadership, their subordinates, and clients.

By far the most meaningful source or bearer of recognition as perceived by the majority of employees is their *immediate manager* or *supervisor*. But the troubling realization is that the majority of employees don't feel recognized by their line managers for their dedication, work practices, or results. What is happening?

Given the importance placed by subordinates to receiving recognition why then aren't line managers giving (enough) recognition to their staff? An explanation could be that people-managers aren't given a lot of support in the way of education, coaching, and encouragement specifically on staff recognition. At the same time there is no accountability placed on line managers for actually giving proper and effective recognition according to some scholars.[61]

Recognition between line managers and their subordinates occurs obviously vertically.

Vertical recognition can be expressed not only between staff and their direct line managers but also between staff and higher-level executives of the organization. Being given recognition directly by an executive can be incredibly motivational. But employees feel that their leaders are less often walking-the-talk, are getting increasingly out of touch with their workforces, and therefore less in a position to give recognition.[62]

Besides vertical recognition between line manager (and executives) and staff, recognition can be expressed horizontally between peers or co-workers. Peer recognition is important because it arguably comes from those in the best position to judge one's job effort or work quality.[63] But we found that most employees don't perceive peer recognition as important as being recognized by immediate line manager.

Employees can also be recognized by their organization which Brun and Dugas call institutional recognition. Institutional recognition consists of policies and programs affirming the organization's commitment to recognizing employees. We found for instance that employees value the offering by the organization of training and development programs as it makes them feel that the organization is investing in them. Employees perceive it as 'I'm doing a good job and you want me to go further'.

Then of course employees can receive external recognition from clients, suppliers and other external stakeholders together with social recognition. *Social recognition* can occur in relationships between the community and employees. Opportunities to 'give back to the community' and 'strive for a better world' through their organization are increasingly perceived as valuable types of recognition by employees. We found that the wider the sources of recognition are translated into meaningful recognition practices within our organizations, the more energies employees will exert not only within their jobs but also in helping realize organizational change. But it is important to reiterate that by far the most important source of recognition as generically perceived by employees is their immediate line manager or supervisor.

5. *How should I be recognized?*

Recognition is expressed in human relationships and is practiced on a daily, regular, or ad hoc basis. It is more effective when personalized and specific. It must be adapted and meaningful to the recipient. Employee recognition can take various forms: spoken, written, material, or symbolic.[64]

We found that the most engaging form of recognition as perceived by the majority of employees is: *individual* as opposed to collective, *private* as opposed to public, *informal* as opposed to formal, *nonmonetary* as opposed to monetary, and directly from line manager or supervisor.[65] Ironically this can often be achieved simply through the sincere, personal, informal, and timely use of only two words … 'thank you'. Unfortunately those simple words 'thank you' can be the hardest words to say for some of us but can mean the very most to those of us who need to hear it.[66]

There can be unintended consequences of formal, public, collective, and even monetary recognition. We found that formal and monetary recognition, for instance, in the form of receiving a company-headed bonus letter by mail, is often perceived by employees as a missed opportunity to engage. Also the perceived value of the monetary amount can disappoint and evoke future reactions like 'there is no point relying on the incentive or bonus to be recognised or recognise your staff'. Furthermore, we found that most employees don't really like public recognition. Most employees don't want to be overly praised in front of other people because of the reactions that such public recognition may evoke among their colleagues. In terms of collective recognition, many employees fail to understand recognizing a team by for instance organizing social functions together after work as it infiltrates too much into their personal time.

Basically we found that employees are not looking for huge accolades or anything like that but just some indication of their efforts being valued. So, it raises the question, 'What does it take for line managers to share some time, show some interest, and express some care?'

6. *When should I be recognized?*

Existential recognition should be expressed *every day* through a host of simple gestures such as warm greetings and sincere thanks as well as symbolically. The exertion of extra-energies to job and organization should be recognized sincerely, informally, and personally as soon as identified. But such off-the-cuff recognition there is not enough of that according to most employees.

In stark contrast to receiving off-the-cuff recognition many employees can't even remember the last time they actually got recognized. If they do remember it was done formally and merely once a year during an annual performance review. Which also brings to question the perceived quality of many of such performance reviews.

7. *What happens if I am not recognized?*

This is what happens: we get withdrawal of energies to job; we get withdrawal of energies to organization; we get individual inertia; we get organizational inertia; we get insight inertia; we get action inertia; we become physically uninvolved; we become cognitively unvigilant; and we become emotionally disconnected.

Not receiving recognition also negatively impacts other key employee related facets since recognition is a carrier of our identity, of our meaning, of our purpose, of our self-esteem, and ultimately of our psychological well-being.

Without an enduring practice of recognition, we surely won't be mobilizing a critical mass of our workforces and realizing any organizational change. So, not recognizing employees for their contributions is simply not an option. There are various ethical, humanistic, existential, psychodynamic, and behavioural reasons as to why employees should be recognized. Not just because there is a business case in it but 'because failing to show gratitude to those who deserve it offends against the norms of society'.[67]

7
Sustaining Organizational Energy

Our journey throughout this book has ultimately been about unleashing *organizational energy* for strategic change efforts to be realized. As explored, the source of energy for people doesn't come from an executive-monopolized plan. The energy comes from personally connecting with a compelling story that has been co-created.

Organizational energy, or the lack of it, is very evident in our business life. Organizations lacking energy are often characterized by inertia, change fatigue, cynicism, organizational burnout, and lack of innovation. Not an ideal scenario for trying to realize any strategic change. It's not difficult to see why positive organizational energy needs to be unleashed... and sustained.

We feel that organizational energy needs to be sustained when it comes to two fundamental areas in particular: our customers and our people. Sustaining true *customer-centricity* and *people-centricity* throughout our strategic change journey always remains a challenge. In this final chapter, we examine how to sustain customer and people centricities. We reflect on how to sustain organizational energy, momentum, and keeping the collective story alive by bringing together some of the key theories, practices, and models explored throughout the book.

Sustaining customer-centricity

This is where it so often goes wrong. We may have gone through the intense practice of unlocking deep customer insights through strategic sensing from the Outside-In. We subsequently may have been able to co-create distinctive strategies together with existing, new and prospective customers. In now trying to implement these customer-centric strategies we often face two challenges. The obvious challenge is that we revert back to being consumed and dealing with the day-to-day operational challenges. And even if we are committed to also realizing our developed strategies we need to be mindful of not slipping back to merely the 'mechanics' of rolling-out our strategic plan. We often find that the focus of leadership teams quickly becomes 'limited' to measuring the implementation progress of the already developed customer plans. We often revert to an internally driven focus on ticking the boxes of our strategic plan. Whilst tracking the accountabilities and reviewing the progress is a necessary discipline, it is still an internally driven process. But we also need to maintain our focus on continued strategic sensing from the Outside-In. Seeing, feeling and thinking from a customer-centric perspective can't be put on hold just because we are busy implementing earlier developed customer strategies. Our markets and customers are not standing still; nor can we.

In need of a Chief Customer Officer?

What we want to avoid is reverting to purely being sales and marketing driven or silo-based views of our customers. This calls for visible and accountable customer-centric leadership starting from the top at C-suite level. But who within the C-suite takes ownership of the customer experience besides the CEO, who typically is inundated with a wide variety of corporate demands?

Isn't it revealing that we typically award C-titles to any internally driven responsibility but not to our customer? Many organizations have a Chief Operations Officer, a Chief Financial Officer, a Chief Risk Officer, a Chief Information Officer or even a Chief Administration Officer. Where is the customer representation at top executive level? In some organizations the customer is represented at this level through a Chief Marketing Officer. But as we contested earlier, being driven by marketing or sales is still an Inside-Out orientation. Also, in most of today's organizations there are many more customer touch-points that lie outside the traditional domain of sales and marketing. These touch-points are opportunities to provide high-value to our customers and achieve differentiation. The customer, of course, is too important to be 'owned' solely by a Chief Marketing Officer or any member of the organization for that matter. But we feel that the customer's voice does need a new champion sitting at the highest levels of power within our organizations.

A few organizations such as Oracle, Microsoft, and Mazda have developed Chief Customer Officer (CCO) roles at senior levels. But the role is still very new. For instance, there are only around 35 CCO roles within *Fortune* 500 companies and only 500 or so roles worldwide, according to the Chief Customer Council.[1] The Council claims that 'the role remains relatively undefined and poorly understood even amongst the C-suite and especially amongst customers. A number of CCOs still have to explain what their role is when they hand over their business card to customers'.

So, what does the CCO role entail? The CCO role is properly defined as 'an executive that provides the comprehensive and authoritative view of the customer and creates corporate and customer strategy at the highest levels of the company to maximize customer acquisition, retention, and profitability' according to the Council. We feel that such a definition is somewhat unfortunate as it comes across as too Inside-Out driven. The driver for a CCO role shouldn't merely be maximizing customer profitability but leveraging joint value. But we agree with the Council that one of the most important roles of the CCO is to help create and sustain a customer-centric culture complete with accountability and ownership at all levels of the organization.

Such a customer-centric culture was lacking at the Boeing Training & Flight Services division. This Boeing division with 1,500 employees serving 500 airline customers in over 90 countries decided to reorganize around the customer.[2] CCO Roei Ganzarski defined the division's breakthrough moment as

> the realisation that, in order to continue growing successfully, we needed to be more focused on our customers than ever before. Our organizational culture wasn't optimal to say the least. Our operations departments were focused on our products and services, our finance teams on collecting payments, and our sales and business development teams on meeting short-term revenue goals. But no one was looking at things from the customers' holistic perspective. We knew we needed to change our culture to better serve the one reason we all exist – our customers.[3]

So, we see the role as a holistic one where the CCO is the ultimate coordinator and facilitator ensuring sustained customer-centricity throughout the organization. The CCO ensures that we sense strategically from the Outside-In at multiple levels, that we keep unlocking deep customer insights, and that we keep co-creating and realizing distinctive strategies together with existing, new and prospective customers. In short, the CCO helps ensure that we don't fall back into internal-functional driven perspectives but sustain a true customer-centric one leveraging value through co-discovery and co-creation. They keep the organization staying focused on driving customer value.

Not the silver bullet

It's important to recognize that a chief customer officer is not a silver bullet for all of our organization's customer experience problems. With the growing interest in customer experience, some CCOs worry that companies will rush too quickly into creating the position before building an environment for them to be successful.[4] Their concern seems well-founded as the CCO role is the most fragile in the C-suite with an average tenure of less than 30 months.[5] Or, as a CCO from a major software company warns: 'I worry about this as a role...it's in vogue and many companies will hire one because they think they need one. In three to five years, I'm afraid we may see lots of flameout because they weren't given the seniority or authority to make a difference'.[6]

Whether organizations call the position Chief Customer Officer or some other label, it is important to remember that these individuals need to serve as top executives with the mandate and power to co-create, orchestrate and improve customer experiences across the ever-more-complex range of customer interactions.[7]

Sustaining critical mass

There are many challenges with sustaining organizational energies. Throughout this book we already explored how to gain critical mass by unleashing combined energies in terms of Can-Know-Want. In other words, how to ensure that we've got people who are capable and proficient, who are aligned and cognitively understand, and who are engaged and emotionally committed to exerting extra-energies.

But it is also important to remember that we need to sustain a *critical mass* of such people unleashing these combined energies.

In social dynamics, critical mass is a sufficient number of adopters of an initiative within a social system so that the rate of adoption becomes self-sustaining and creates further growth.[8] If we don't manage to exceed such a threshold of adaptors within our organization no strategic change effort will be sustained.

Clearly we need a critical mass among *all* of our people. But such a threshold is more likely to be gained by unleashing the Can-Know-Want energies of certain employee groups who then influence others within the organization. Consider, for instance, that roughly 60% to 70% of our workforce is led by first-line managers. So, it does surprise us that executives rarely identify *first-line employee segments* that are of crucial importance to help gaining a wider critical mass across their organizations. For instance, nursing unit managers are a vital employee segment for healthcare organizations, supervisors for mining companies, officers for emergency services organizations, or store managers for retail companies. These employee segments are of such strategic importance in helping executives mobilize the wider workforce. Failing to gain a critical mass among such a crucial employee segment inevitably means failure of realizing any organizational change effort. Yet, we rarely come across specific first-line programs focussed on unleashing the combined energies of these vital employee segments.

Sustaining combined energies at *multiple levels*

Another key challenge worth highlighting relates to not only gaining a critical mass of people exerting combined Can-Know-Want energies but also at *multiple levels*. In other words, exerting these combined energies not merely at job level but also at divisional level and critically at organizational level. We believe that Figure 7.1 reflects the enormity of such a challenge. For organizational change to be sustained, a critical mass of combined energies needs to be mobilized across *all* nine boxes. There simply are no exceptions.

Let's examine further. When launching the organizational strategy, executives are quick to expect people to support it and exert energies to making it happen. But for the bottom-right quadrant in Figure 7.1

	Can (Strategically proficient)	Know (Strategically aligned)	Want (Strategically engaged)
Individual level	**Individual Job Proficiency** Possesses the right competencies & skills to fulfil core strategic change-requirements of the job	**Individual Job Alignment** Cognitively understands and responds to strategic change-requirements within individual's own job	**Individual Job Engagement** Initiates strategic change and exerts extra-energies for the betterment of individual's own job
Group level	**Group Task Proficiency** Is able to fulfil the prescribed strategic change-requirements of the group	**Group Strategic Alignment** Cognitively understands and is strategically aligned with change-requirements of the Group	**Group Strategic Engagement** Initiates or supports strategic change and exerts extra-energies for the betterment of the group
Organizational level	**Organizational Task Proficiency** Can fulfil the prescribed strategic change-requirements of the organization	**Organizational Strategic Alignment** Cognitively understands and is strategically aligned with change-requirements of the organization	**Organizational Strategic Engagement** Initiates or supports strategic change and exerts extra-energies for the betterment of the organization

Figure 7.1 The challenge: a critical mass of people exerting combined energies (Can-Know-Want) and at multiple levels (individual-group-organizational)

to become a reality, many conditions need to be met first. These basic conditions seem obvious but again are rarely met.

For instance, how can we expect people to be engaged at organizational level when a critical mass aren't equipped with the right resources, skills, and competencies to fulfil the requirements be it at individual, departmental or organizational levels? It's amazing to find how often people are expected to realize new strategic requirements with only existing operational capabilities and resources. Or, people may well be strategically proficient but they don't cognitively understand the strategic change requirements at the various levels. In this case, executives failed to contextualize the organizational strategy at departmental and individual levels. And even if a critical mass of the workforce were to be strategically proficient and aligned at the multiple levels, the moment they aren't engaged at individual job level, all is lost as our own research indicates.

No other energies will do!

Let's remind ourselves of what happens if we don't sustain Can-Know-Want energies at multiple levels. In other words, if we fail to sustain productive organizational energies. What does indeed happen when

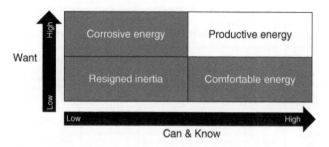

Figure 7.2 The challenge: avoiding redirection of productive energy into comfortable energy, corrosive energy, or resigned inertia

Source: Adapted from the work of Bruch and Vogel (2011).[9]

our strategic change effort runs out of energy and simply fades away? What happens when our collective strategic change effort hits a plateau at some level?

What happens is that the productive organizational energy that we so painfully have been co-creating rapidly can be redirected into either comfortable energy, corrosive energy, or resigned inertia, as illustrated in Figure 7.2. So, dependent on the combination of the Want-dimension with the Can & Know-dimension different energy states can exist within our organizations. Let's briefly examine further.

The 'size-of-the-prize' is of course sustaining the top-right quadrant or *productive energy*. This state means that we are maintaining to mobilize a critical mass of Can-Know-Want energies towards realizing our shared compelling story. People collectively show enthusiasm, high levels of shared alertness and apply an intensely focused change effort to their job, their department, and the wider organization.[10] This state doesn't mean that we all need to be operating at a constant high. That would simply not be sustainable. Productive energy can be decelerated when needed but the point to remember is that it's about maintaining positive energy. This is in contrast with the other three organizational states that in our view display negative energies.

Clearly, what we need to avoid is losing the strategic engagement of our People or the Want. When people don't Want to see and think differently anymore, they retract to a 'North view'. The moment this happens we have digressed into a *comfortable energy* state. Even though people Can and Know how to fulfil typical strategic change requirements, they have become comfortable with the status quo. Technically, comfortable energy is seen as a positive state by academics since people are satisfied, feel at ease, and identify with the status quo.[11] But we do view it as negative especially in relation to strategic change. We feel that the status quo can never be comfortable. Throughout this book we already explored in-depth the monkey-trap example. We explored how organizations lulled by their past successes stop questioning the status quo and lose their alertness, passion and readiness to go to the limits. Instead, when comfortable energy becomes dominant, organizations become complacent, lazy or arrogant with detrimental consequences.

What we also need to avoid is for productive energy to become *corrosive energy*. In this state people may Want to exert energies but are starting to realize that they don't possess the right skills or don't have the right resources (Can't) or aren't aligned (Don't Know) to fulfil the organizational change requirements. The originally established productive energy is redirected into destructive energy. Organizations with corrosive energy often show high levels of aggression, anger and fury according to academics. They describe it as a state of 'high alertness and creativity to harm others inside the organization; destructive internal conflicts and micro-political activities. In other words, any tendencies of units or teams to weaken another unit in favour of maximizing own interests ultimately confirm corrosive energy'.[12]

The 'death warmed-up' state is that of *resigned inertia*. We no longer have a critical mass of people who not only Can and Know but most importantly who Want. Large parts of the organization are emotionally withdrawing and openly showing indifference to company goals. Various change initiatives have failed and people don't feel conviction about, or meaning in, yet another strategic change initiative. They are left feeling apathetic to change. In this resigned state there is widespread action-inertia and insight-inertia as discussed in Chapter 6.

Sustaining momentum

During the 34th America's Cup, Team New Zealand looked poised to sail away with little resistance. With an 8–1 lead, the New Zealand team only needed one more win to clinch the Cup while the US team needed eight consecutive wins in the first-to-nine series. Having just lost the eighth race, Jimmy Spithil, the US team skipper, walked into the press room and dared to declare to the world media 'We can win races, we're not done. This could be the greatest comeback in sailing'.[13] And amazingly, the US team went on to win eight races straight to complete one of the most famous comebacks in the event's 162-year history. Team New Zealand had thrown away a seven-race lead to lose the America's Cup. Depending on the perspective, it is either the ultimate comeback story or the ultimate example of losing momentum. After having done everything right and leading eight races to one, the momentum seemed to have left the New Zealand boat after narrowly missing out on a decisive ninth race win.

The America's Cup example of losing momentum is emblematic for organizational life as well. 'The project lost momentum. That is the long and the short of it. We had it in our hands. There was no way that I thought they could get to market before us. We had the people, the direction, but somehow, it just slipped away. We shouldn't have gotten sidetracked ... We took our eye off the ball and let it slip away'.[14] Many of us in organizational life probably have heard or said something to the same effect. Imagine going through the effort of trying to realize distinctive strategic change by co-creating a compelling story as described throughout this book. Imagine mobilizing people to see, feel, think, plan, and act differently. Imagine gaining a critical mass of people who Can, Know and Want to support the strategic change at multiple levels throughout the organization. Imagine having unleashed all of this productive organizational energy only to lose momentum and jeopardize the whole effort. Not sustaining momentum and winning eight out of the nine races left Team New Zealand with nothing. Equally, gaining a critical mass of support by co-creating a compelling story and distinctive strategies can count for nothing. The unleashed productive energy can quickly digress into corrosive or comfortable energy and eventually resigned inertia.

The challenge of keeping the ball rolling

Gaining a critical *mass* or threshold per se is not enough because the mass also needs to be (and stay) in motion. That is why *momentum* can defined as the force of motion, or alternatively, the force or energy associated with a moving mass.[15] In physics, momentum is a cornerstone concept referring to mass and velocity.[16] As mass gains velocity it gains momentum. Think of a ball rolling down a hill gaining speed as it rolls. But in a social change context, the challenge of keeping the ball rolling is challenging because the ball doesn't always move in a straight or linear downhill trajectory. Even though our originally defined strategic trajectory may well be clear, 'just' persisting with or trying to extend this expected trajectory often will not suffice. In other words, the ball won't always be able to move in a linear fashion. Or, the energy we direct at sustaining our current defined trajectory may well have to be redirected, replaced, or overcome by a momentum in a new direction. We need to keep the ball rolling but also may need to have to change our anticipated direction. This means we may well have to change aspects of our compelling story and our originally co-created strategies. And this means that a critical mass of people have to be redirected. All of this makes sustaining momentum so challenging.

The three dimensions of momentum

So, we are back at deeper examining momentum in relation to the three dimensions: Can, Know and Want. Figure 7.3 looks incredibly straightforward but let's not be deceived by its simplicity.

Again, in terms of the *Can-momentum* dimension, we can't expect people to realize strategic change with existing operational capabilities. So, equipping people with the right resources at multiple

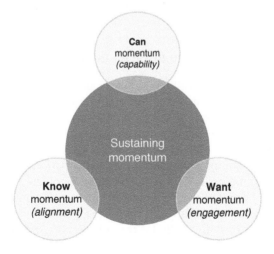

Figure 7.3 The three dimensions of momentum

levels is surprisingly an often-overlooked 'hygiene' factor. But ensuring capabilities at the start of the strategic initiative may not be enough to sustain momentum. As already highlighted, the originally intended strategic direction may well have to be fine-tuned or even redirected during the course. This often means that we need to update or secure different capabilities and resources to sustain the Can-momentum. Again, sounds basic but often overlooked. The same logic applies to sustaining *Know-momentum*. Strategy is never linear and there always will be modifications. But people need understand these strategic modifications at multiple levels and stay cognitively involved. Most difficult to sustain is the *Want-momentum* or maintaining strategic engagement across the organization. In other words, keeping people emotionally committed throughout our strategic change journey despite the inevitable disruptions and modifications along the way. People who are engaged at the start of a strategic change program can become disengaged along the way when exposed to various modifications and disruptions to the original strategic plans. Especially, when people feel they haven't been communicated, let alone engaged, about certain strategic changes that have a direct impact on them personally. We feel there is an untapped opportunity, beyond just updating employees, to offer them a sensemaking-platform and continue gaining their insights, feedback and engagement through social media. Let's explore further.

Sustaining energy through social media

There is a bigger opportunity for more organizations, we feel, to enduringly mobilize employees for strategic change through social media. 'Texting, tweeting, blogging, tagging, posting videos and uploading photos are the mainstream methods for communication in today's society.'[17] Logic would dictate that most organizations would be dialoguing and sensemaking with their employees using similar social methods. But the use of social media for most organizations has been 'limited' to engaging an external audience. 'Little time has been spent on how this interactive platform can be used to engage a workforce internally for the collaboration and benefit of a business'.[18]

As the workforce becomes ever more engaged with social media, our organizational leaders must keep pace as well, as stated in a recent EY report. Engaging our employees in strategic change efforts through traditional 'communication' methods will no longer suffice. Especially, when we realize that the demographics of our workforces are shifting so dramatically. For instance, Millennials, or Generation Y, are entering the workforce in greater numbers and are projected to make up 75 per cent of the global workforce by 2025, according to a recent Deloitte Global Human Capital Trends report.[19] Millennials are 'expected to have different behaviors, values and attitudes as a response to the technological and economic implications of the internet'.[20]

So, we feel there is a big opportunity for organizational leaders to interact and capitalize on gaining insights and feedback from their employees through social media.

Sustaining leadership orchestration

The common theme in this chapter about sustaining organizational energy, customer centricity, critical mass, and momentum has to be committed leadership. People do not follow uncommitted leaders. It is as simple as that. Yet it is a key reason why so many strategies fail. It is often the lack of sustained commitment from the CEO and executive team themselves! There is a danger of it all becoming too hard and many of the individual executive members retracting to their own functional silos. This is triggered when executive members don't see their own CEO completely devoted to sustaining the strategic cause. But there is no half-way as 'only one who devotes himself to a cause with his whole strength and soul can be a true master. For this reason mastery demands all of a person', as Albert Einstein said.[21] The knock-on effect is that the wider workforce withdraws their extra-energies from realizing the organizational strategy to merely fulfilling their operational job requirements. Realizing strategic change enduringly truly demands *all* of the CEO, the executive team, and leaders throughout the organization.

It is a big demand and indeed there is nothing easy about what we are asking organizational leaders to be and do. In a way, we feel that they need to be the ultimate orchestrators. What do we mean by *orchestrating*?

Orchestrating, to us, is not simply taken as coordinating some strategic resources and processes. What we mean by orchestrating is for organizational leaders to connect energetically the practices of Sensing, Co-creating, Realizing, Recognizing, and Behaving. These practices have been explored throughout this book and are illustrated in a simplified model in Figure 7.4. Without overly expanding on each of the already explored practices, we instead examine the *workings* of our orchestration model. And whilst the model is simplified, it does highlight the considerable and continued devotion required from leaders.

A well-orchestrated organization naturally sets in motion an energetic swirl that continuously updates each of the practices and rejuvenates the organizational strategy as a whole. Orchestrating for strategic change is a big effort because *all* practices need to be linked

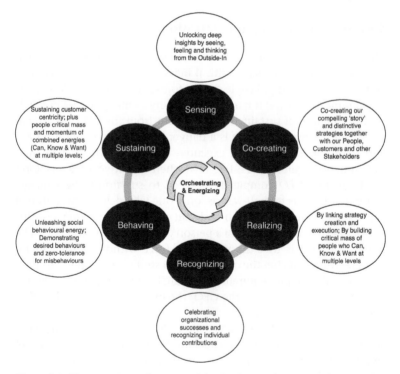

Figure 7.4   The practices of sustained leadership orchestration for strategic change

and kept reinforced by organizational leaders for the energetic swirl to stay in motion. Let's explore the linked practices.

Leaders constantly need to reinforce *Sensing* as it protects our organization from reverting to an Inside-Out or product-driven perspective, as explored in Chapter 2. In reference to earlier metaphors used in that chapter, Sensing prevents us from being trapped within our 'North-view' and allows us to unlock deep insights and 'D-options'. A continuously reinforced Sensing through seeing, feeling, and thinking from the Outside-In prevents us from living on past glories and the dangers of 'holding-on-to-the-nut'. To make sure the Sensing swirl stays in motion, leaders will need to keep actively orchestrating them.

Co-creation of distinctive strategies also needs continuous reinforcement because strategy development can never stop or be periodic. Our external environment is too volatile and strategies therefore need to be updated or transformed on an ongoing basis so that our strategies remain distinctive at any point of time, as examined in Chapter 5. Strategy development can't be monopolized either by the executives. Instead, executives have to reinforce the need for continued co-creation with the various stakeholders. All of this takes up a lot of prolonged energy and reinforcement of people centricities. As we discussed in Chapter 3, an important way to do this is by keeping alive our co-created compelling 'story'. Again, this is achieved not through periodic top-down 'communication' but continual sense-making and dialogue at multiple levels of our organization.

Another important orchestrating task when it comes to *Realizing* our strategy isn't just viewing *execution* as a consequential step after the *development* phase but to actually link the practices of co-creation and execution, as suggested in Chapter 5. Again, there are so many fast changing variables impacting on our strategies necessitating the orchestration or a continuous back-and-forth practice of strategic sensing, co-creation, and execution. This back-and-forth activity of the inter-connected practices ensures momentum. It also facilitates the continued focus on enabling a critical mass of people who Can, Know and Want at multiple levels of the organization, as discussed in this chapter.

All of this continued orchestration of strategic sensing, co-creation, and execution is jeopardized when it comes to *Behaving*. More precisely, all our efforts are jeopardized the moment we start accepting and rewarding high performance regardless of the display of undesired behaviours, as highlighted in Chapter 1. Leadership will have to demonstrate zero-tolerance when it comes to misbehaviours, including from high performing people. When misbehaviours are tolerated we start losing our social energy which then quickly turns into corrosive energy. Only a continued reinforcement of our desired behaviours and decisive action in relation to misbehaviours sustains social energy that provides meaning, direction and mobilization.

Finally, our dynamic practice of orchestrating and continuous renewal only comes full circle with continuously *Recognizing* people for their contributions. Feeling recognized is the single most critical driver for people to exert extra-energies for the betterment of the wider organization, as explored in Chapter 6. The most meaningful source of recognition as perceived by employees is their immediate manager or supervisor. So, executives will need to continuously reinforce to their people-managers the importance of recognizing staff on an individual basis sincerely, timely, and personally. Because remember what happens if this is not done: we get withdrawal of energies to job; we get withdrawal of energies to organization; we get individual inertia; we get organizational inertia; we get insight inertia; we get action inertia; people become physically uninvolved; people become cognitively unvigilant; and people become emotionally disconnected.

It is impossible to capture the in-depth explorations of this book within a single model. But our final model in Figure 7.4 hopefully does highlight the required devotion of leaders to continuously orchestrating and energizing the strategic practices of Sensing, Co-creating, Realizing, Behaving, and Recognizing. This is on top of keeping the show going, or in other words, on top of managing our day-to-day operational challenges.

We also want to reiterate the importance of not 'merely' orchestrating each of the practices individually but in terms of each other. Renewing each practice on its own may temporarily move our organization ahead but eventually will leave it vulnerable to competitors catching up. Only an organization that orchestrates these practices continuously and simultaneously generates true momentum and competitive advantage. As soon as this momentum is interrupted because leadership focuses on one or two practices to the neglect of the others, standstill looms, our strategic change effort is jeopardized, and competitors are given the chance to catch up.

Perhaps Jack Welch said it best when he stated, 'I've always believed that when the rate of change inside an institution becomes slower than the rate of change outside, the end is in sight. The only question is when'.[22] Sustained leadership orchestration in terms of continuous inter-linkage and renewal of our described practices ensures the organization moves ahead of the market...enduringly.

Afterword

We are humbled that you took the time to get to know the insights of this book. We wrote the book with one conviction and one purpose: to solve the strategy delusion. We live in a world of such volatility, uncertainty, complexity and ambiguity that we no longer can afford to remain 'delusional' about making strategy happen.

Through this book, we have tried to solve the strategy delusion *not* by providing the 'answers' but to help make possible different practices. In other words, different ways of seeing, feeling, thinking, planning, and acting when it comes to realizing strategy. There are no simple or correct answers to 'the canon of strategy' as expressively described by Kevin Roberts in the Foreword. Strategy can never be seen as a tick-the-box-exercise with right and wrong answers.

So, our purpose has been to inspire you with conceptual and practical insights that may unleash new energies in yourself and your colleagues on your strategy journey. Remember that this book may serve only as the beginning of that journey. The real journey and fulfilment for you and your team will come from realizing your intended strategy, together. If, on that journey, you take just a few points from this book, take those.

Before embarking on any strategy journey, make sure to *surround yourself with disciples*. Establish an A-team equipped not just with operational proficiency but also with strategic capability, strategic understanding, and strategic engagement to leading and realizing distinctive organizational strategies.

Then start *letting go of the nut*. Don't hold on to the status quo, to ingrained organizing models, to 20th-century leadership styles, to conventional strategic thinking, to periodic and monopolized planning, or to new versions of old strategies.

Instead, start *sensing and co-creating from the Outside-In*. Unlock deep customer insights through seeing, feeling and thinking from their perspective first. Be customer-value driven as opposed to product, sales or marketing driven. Co-create distinctive strategies together with existing, new and prospective customers, and also other stakeholders. Don't forget to link sensing, creation and realization into one continuous strategic practice.

Don't even attempt to mobilize people with a 70-page strategic plan. Instead, commit to *co-creation of a compelling story* as explored in this book. Gain a critical mass of people at multiple levels who are proficient (Can), who are aligned (Know), and who are emotionally committed (Want) to realizing strategic change.

Don't just inform people about organizational change efforts through conventional corporate 'communication'. But engage them through deeper *dialogue and sensemaking* throughout the organization. Also, gain deep insights and feedback by interacting with your employees through social media.

Make sure to *unleash energy through behaviours*. Hold people accountable to be high performers *and* demonstrate desired behaviours. Exhibit zero-tolerance of misbehaviours, including from high performing people. Reinforce desired behaviours and take decisive action in relation to misbehaviours. Such action will guard the social energy that provides meaning, direction and mobilization.

Recognize at individual level. Recognize employees for their contributions. Individual recognition is the most critical driver for the exertion of extra-energies as perceived by employees. Remember that the most meaningful source of recognition is their immediate manager or supervisor. So, reinforce to people-managers the importance of recognizing their staff sincerely, timely, and personally.

Finally and vitally, *sustain leadership orchestration*. Devote yourself and your A-team to orchestrating the practices of Sensing, Co-creating, Realizing, Recognizing, and Behaving. This means continuously and simultaneously inter-linking and renewing all of these practices, not just one or two. Such sustained leadership orchestration of all practices ensures the organization moves ahead of the market ... enduringly.

Please note that the above points are obviously simplified for the purpose of this epilogue and merely touch on *what* our key arguments are. *Why* these points are so critical and *how* they can be realized has been explored, in-depth, throughout this book. That's why *Solving the Strategy Delusion* doesn't belong on your bookshelf. It belongs on your desk! We hope that it can serve as an indispensable point of reference for you and your team. Should you need any additional information, we are only a few keystrokes away at www.criticalmanagement.com. au. We wish you all the best on your strategy journey.

Marc Stigter
Mornington Peninsula, Australia

Sir Cary Cooper
Lancaster, UK

Glossary

Note: Most definitions given in this glossary are not academic in nature but make practical reference to what has been developed in this book. They are defined in the context of strategic change and are intended to facilitate reading.

Action intuition   Relates to the ability to not just think but also *feel* how strategies can be realized. The ability, for instance, to not merely understand but also feel like a customer – or customer empathy – is directly linked to action intuition.

Action inertia   The withdrawal of extra-energies by employees to realizing strategic change.

Chief Customer Officer (CCO)   An executive who is the ultimate coordinator and facilitator ensuring sustained customer-centricity throughout the organization. A CCO ensures that the organization senses strategically from the Outside-In at multiple levels; that it keeps unlocking deep customer insights; and that it keeps co-creating and realizing distinctive strategies together with existing, new and prospective customers. A CCO keeps the organization staying focused on driving customer value.

Cohesion   Within a people context, is about team bonding and about what keeps any group together. It is a level of affective connection to each other.

Counterproductive behaviours   Voluntary behaviour of organizational members that violates significant organizational norms and in doing so threatens the well-being of the organization and its members.

Collaboration   The extent to which members work together towards co-creating and realizing the strategic change. It also considers the nature of the dialogue in which members determine together what the strategic priorities are and how best to action them.

Collectiveness   The extent to which everyone in the entity strategically acts as a whole and is viewed as one.

Comfortable energy   An organizational state where people *Can* and *Know* but don't *Want* to realize distinctive strategies as they have become comfortable with business-as-usual. Lulled by the organization's past successes they have stopped questioning the status quo and have lost their alertness, passion and readiness to go to the limits. Instead, when comfortable energy becomes dominant, organizations become complacent, lazy or arrogant with detrimental consequences.

Compassion   Relates to feelings of empathy to other members of the team. It is not merely understanding their qualms, fears or anguishes but feeling these as if one has experienced them oneself.

Compelling story   For people to make sense of a strategic plan it needs to go beyond the specifics of the plan itself but be part of a collective 'story' ultimately comprising of seven 'simple' questions: 1) What are our desired behaviours? 2) Where have we come from? 3) Where are we today and what is our reason for being? 4) What does success look like by when? 5) How do we (need to) add value to whom? 6) What are our key focus areas and priorities? and 7) What is the individual employee's role in turning our story into reality?

Concurrency   The extent to which members of the team or organization step up at the same time to actively champion and lead the strategic change.

Congruence   Refers to *values*-congruence or the homogeneity between individual and team or organizational values. It also refers to *goal*-congruence or the extent that individuals perceive their own goals as being satisfied by the accomplishment of the team's or organizational strategic goals

Corrosive energy   An organizational state where people may *Want* to exert energies but are starting to realize that they don't possess the right skills or don't have the right resources (*Can't*) or aren't aligned (*Don't Know*) to fulfil the organizational change requirements. Organizations with corrosive energy often show high levels of destructive internal conflicts and micro-political activities.

Corporate anorexia   The pursuit of 'knee-jerk' cost-cutting and downsizing in today's economic climate typically seen as a rational strategy and as cloned and learned responses to uncertainty.

Critical mass   A sufficient number of adopters of an initiative within a social system so that the rate of adoption becomes self-sustaining and creates further growth. If executives don't manage to exceed such a threshold of adaptors within their organization, no strategic change effort will be sustained.

Dialogue   The medium through which people seek shared meaning and understanding. Dialogue not only can increase sensemaking and the affective commitment of people to change but it also adds value through people's enhancements of originally proposed strategies.

D-option   Part of analogy used in this book to symbolize the creation of novel and distinctive strategies from the Outside-In as opposed to conventional A-B-C strategies from the Inside-Out

Empathy shift   Ability to abandon one's own logic based on own perspective and see (and feel) from others' perspectives.

Entrepreneurial sensing   The innate ability to sense for opportunities through seeing, feeling and thinking differently from the Outside-In or external perspective and without feeling limited by resources currently controlled.

Individual inertia   The withdrawal of extra-energies and the resistance of *individual* employees to help realizing organizational change.

Inside sensing   Insights are detected mainly from within our own paradigm and based on linear and analytical thought. In this rational state, sensing though feeling or intuition is not really applied. This state is mostly internally driven and strategic seeing is limited to our own perspective.

Inside creation   Strategies are developed mainly in isolation of customers. This approach is not customer centric but internal and products driven. Customers are traditionally perceived as 'targets' and as passive recipients of products or services. The relationship is transactional and our main driver is simply to increase sales.

Inside-Out sensing   Trying to some extent analyse the external environment and detect insights but these still influenced by our own paradigm. External insights are selected that 'prove' own preconceived hypotheses. In this state, not a lot of strategic intuition is applied and strategies are mainly based on rational and linear thought.

Inside-Out creation   This approach still relies on what the organization conventionally thinks the customers' needs are. Sources of insights are based largely on periodic surveys and mining of CRM databases. Strategies are often driven and created from the Inside-Out without involvement of customers. They are created *for* not *with* customers.

Insight   A sudden and unexpected strategic solution arrived at after an impasse has been reached and an incubation period has elapsed. An incubation period is often necessary for insight to occur because it enables non-conscious processes to operate more freely by relaxing constraints imposed by rational analysis

Insight inertia   A state where cues from external and internal environments aren't observed and interpreted in time to determine and adjust organizational behaviour to meet market, customer, and internal demands for strategic change.

Internal outsiders   Non-mainstream thinkers or across-the-grain thinkers or mavericks. They are people already within the organization who see, feel and think differently and who can transform tradition-bound organizations.

Intersection moment   These occur when parties and concepts from one field are brought into new and unfamiliar territory. Or, where established perspectives clash and come together with insights from other disciplines and cultures potentially resulting in an 'explosion' of new paradigms and innovation.

Leadership   Orchestrating and mobilizing people who *Can, Know,* and *Want* to create and realize a preferred direction.

Mission   A strategic concentration that has to shift over a period of time as market and customer conditions change. A good mission should answer the question: *What* do we do and how do we add value to *whom* with what kind of offering *where?*

Mobilizing people   Gaining a critical mass of people who *Can* (capable), who *Know* (aligned), and who *Want* (engaged) to realize organizational strategic change.

Monkey-trap   Part of analogy used in this book to symbolize how organizations or groups of people tend to hold on to the status quo or business-as-usual missing out on opportunities.

Monopolized planning   Stems from the misconception held by many organizational executives that strategies are to be developed during periodic planning sessions and that they are to be formulated mainly by *them.*

Momentum   The force of motion, or alternatively, the force or energy associated with a moving mass.

North view   Part of analogy used in this book to symbolize how organizations or groups of people united by common beliefs or purpose try and make sense of a new situation based on their own 'limited' experiences and preconceived beliefs.

Opportunity intuition Relates to *feeling what* the future direction needs to be from the Outside-in. It relates to the openness and ability to discover opportunities resulting from non-conscious and holistic sensing. Entrepreneurial managers often possess opportunistic intuition and are able to *feel beyond* as opposed to merely *see ahead*. The latter foresees an expected future by constructing a framework out of the events of the past. The former, sensing beyond, constructs the future itself and a world that would not otherwise be.

Orchestration Organizational leaders energetically connecting the strategic practices of Sensing, Co-creating, Realizing, Recognizing, and Behaving. A well-orchestrated organization continuously updates each of the practices and rejuvenates the organizational strategy as a whole. Orchestrating for strategic change is a big effort because *all* practices need to be linked and kept reinforced by organizational leaders.

Organizational citizenship behaviour Employee behaviours of benefit to the wider organization that go beyond the basic requirements of the job and are to a large extent discretionary. These behaviours are critical to facilitating organizational strategic change.

Organizational inertia The resistance of a critical mass of people to realizing organizational strategic change by withdrawing extra-energies.

Organizational misbehaviour Simply described as anything people do at work that they are not supposed to do including the widest range of behaviour from failure to work very hard or conscientiously, through not working at all, deliberate output restriction, practical joking, pilferage, sabotage, or sexual misconduct according to scholars.

Organizational purpose Explains the organization's fundamental reason for existence. An organizational purpose is more enduring and goes much deeper than a particular strategic mission. An organizational purpose typically outlasts planning cycles of developed visions, missions and strategic objectives. A shared and authentic purpose creates a deeper sense of meaning, identity and belonging for people as it encompasses the creation of not only organizational and customer value but typically also the creation of societal or environmental value. In other words a shared purpose is critical because it offers people a wider and common sense of *why* the organization exists.

Outside-In creation   Strategies are co-created together with existing, new and prospective customers. In this externally centric practice the aim is to leverage joint value through co-discovering deep insights and co-creating distinctive strategies together with our customers. Insights are gained as part of a continuous practice of dialogue and sensemaking both qualitatively and virtually.

Outside-In sensing   Starting point for sensing is externally driven from a customer, market and stakeholder perspectives first. Not from an internally driven resources or capabilities perspectives. In this state, insights are unlocked through non-linear thinking.

Productive energy   An organizational state where a critical mass of people *Can, Know* and *Want* to exert extra-energies to making strategic change happen at multiple levels throughout the organization.

Psychological contract   The perceptions of both the individual and the organization of the reciprocal promises and obligations implied in the employment relationship. These promises and obligations represent a set of beliefs regarding the relationship between the individual and the organization. These beliefs are based on perceptions and therefore exist in the eye of the beholder or in the minds of the parties.

Psychological contract violation   An extreme breach of psychological contract often resulting in strong affective responses such as feelings of injustice, betrayal, and deeper psychological distress whereby the victim experiences anger, resentment, a sense of wrongful harm. It can also evoke other extreme emotions such as disillusion, bitterness, bereavement, indignation, hate, and outrage.

Psychological well-being   The extent to which we experience a positive sense of purpose at work. Positive psychological well-being at work means that people are inspired, determined and enthusiastic to not only doing their job but to exerting extra-energies for the organization. Psychological well-being is an affective state and fundamental in mobilizing people for strategic change.

Prozac leadership   Term symbolizing executives with overly 'positive' leadership practices that glorify an exposure to risk.

Recognition A constructive and genuine feedback based on acknowledging people's performance, contributions, dedication and engagement. Recognition is engaged in on a regular or ad hoc basis, and expressed formally or informally, individually or collectively, privately or publicly, and monetarily or non-monetarily.

Resigned inertia A state where the organization no longer has a critical mass of people who, not only *Can* and *Know*, but importantly who *Want*. Large parts of the organization are emotionally withdrawing and openly showing indifference to company goals. Various change initiatives have failed and people don't feel conviction about, or meaning in, yet another strategic change initiative. They are left feeling apathetic to change.

Reward A formal, impartial, and equitable exchange. A material or financial expression of appreciation that is conditional on results.

Sensegiving The process of attempting to influence the sensemaking and meaning construction of others toward a preferred redefinition of organizational reality.

Sensemaking A narrative process by which people attribute meaning to unknown or unexpected events. Sensemaking enables workforces to exchange their experiences and interpretations of such events. It is an important process in mobilizing a critical mass of people because strategic change ultimately is dialogued into existence.

Social exchange contract A contract constructed between companies and their consumer communities in which companies offer consumers resources and a platform to create new services or products and where consumers in return offer companies their insights, skills and time.

Social intuition The social ability to not merely understand but *feel* what the important drivers are from a true People's perspective. Such people-empathy helps with mobilizing a critical mass of the workforce willing to go the extra-mile and exert extra-energies to making strategic change happen.

Strategic delusion Embedded beliefs about Change, Planning, Leadership, Customers, People, and Behaviours with which we tend to be preoccupied and to which we firmly hold despite the non-sensicality of these beliefs.

Strategic drift The tendency for strategies to be developed incrementally on the basis of the dominant logic of businesses but failing to keep pace with a changing environment.

Strategic planning   A periodic process of prioritizing developed strategic objectives and linking them to quantifiable actions, measurements, timings and accountabilities. A misconception held by many executives is that distinctive strategies are to be developed during periodic planning sessions.

Strategy linkage   The removal of the imaginary line between strategy creation and strategy execution by linking these into a *continuous* back-and-forth practice.

Strategy practice   The continuous practice of seeing, feeling and thinking differently from the Outside-In where strategies are co-created with internal and external stakeholders involving collective dialogue and sensemaking.

Strategic sensing   The practice of discovering insights through seeing, feeling and thinking strategically.

Values   Beliefs about standards of behaviour that people agree on demonstrating to achieve the organizational goals. Consistent demonstration of shared values through agreed behaviours provides a source of alignment, motivation, commitment and loyalty among the workforce. Values represent the nucleus of an organization or the DNA of the culture. All organizational behaviours orbit around values.

Visioning   The practice of visioning encompasses the following: 1) The initial and ongoing envisioning of an image of a desired future organizational state in the longer term, through 2) seeing, feeling and thinking about that desired state from the Outside-In, where 3) the collective sensemaking of the vision serves to create a driving force for shared direction, cohesion and mobilization.

Notes

1 What's Going On?

1. http://www.britannica.com/EBchecked/topic/156888/delusion
2. Composite data from the following sources indicate that between 70% and 90% of (strategic) change programs fail: Hoverstadt, P. (2008) *The Fractal Organization: Creating Sustainable Organizations with the Viable System Model*, Chichester, West Sussex: John Wiley & Sons; Higgs, M. and Rowland, D. (2005) 'All Changes Great and Small: Exploring Approached to Change and Its Leadership', *Journal of Change Management*, 5 (2): 121–151; Miller D. (2002) 'Successful Change Leaders: What Makes Them? What Do They Do That Is Different?', *Journal of Change Management*, 2 (4): 359–368; Kotter, J.P. (1995) 'Leading Change: Why Transformation Efforts Fail', *Harvard Business Review*; Decker, P. et al. (2012) 'Predicting Implementation Failure in Organization Change', *Journal of Organizational Culture, Communications and Conflict*, 16 (2): 29–49; Bunres, B. and Jackson, P. (2011) 'Success and Failure in Organizational Change: An Exploration of the Role of Values', *Journal of Change Management*, 11 (2): 133–162.
3. http://www.youtube.com/watch?v=IHdJVzYBBOU
4. http://www.afr.com/p/technology/next_nokia_insider_who_knows_why_Z8at1lqZLp3mAutUO0ye0H
5. Kodak reference see: http://en.wikipedia.org/wiki/Eastman_Kodak; Blockbuster reference see: http://en.wikipedia.org/wiki/Blockbuster_LLC#Online_rentals; *The New York Times* reference see: *The Australian* on 7 August 2013: page 19; Nokia reference see: http://www.bbc.com/news/technology-23947212; BlackBerry reference see: http://bits.blogs.nytimes.com/2014/02/12/blackberrys-market-share-falls-below-others/?_php=true&_type=blogs&_r=0, http://business.time.com/2013/09/24/the-fatal-mistake-that-doomed-blackberry/; Dell reference see: http://en.wikipedia.org/wiki/Market_share_of_personal_computer_vendors and http://www.forbes.com/sites/connieguglielmo/2013/10/30/you-wont-have-michael-dell-to-kick-around-anymore/
6. Adapted from: Bryan, L. and Joyce, C. (2007) *Mobilizing Minds: Creating Wealth from Talent in the 21st-Century Organization*, New York, NY: McGraw-Hill.
7. Ibid.
8. Ibid.
9. http://performance.ey.com/wp-content/uploads/downloads/2014/02/EY-Performance-Using-social-media1.pdf
10. http://performance.ey.com/2014/02/20/using-social-media-engage-workforce/

11. http://performance.ey.com/wp-content/uploads/downloads/2014/02/ EY-Performance-Using-social-media1.pdf
12. Adaptedfrom:http://performance.ey.com/wp-content/uploads/downloads/ 2014/02/EY-Performance-Using-social-media1.pdf
13. http://www.brynmawr.edu/businessworkshops/management/documents/Lencioni-Makeyourvaluesmeansomething.pdf
14. http://www.forbes.com/sites/stevedenning/2012/04/26/jack-welch-ge-the-corporate-practice-of-public-hangings/
15. Ibid.
16. Adapted from Ibid.
17. http://hbr.org/2006/06/growth-as-a-process/ar/1
18. http://www.forbes.com/sites/stevedenning/2012/04/26/jack-welch-ge-the-corporate-practice-of-public-hangings/
19. http://www.sagepub.com/upm-data/9432_010384ch3.pdf
20. http://www.goodreads.com/quotes/70385-the-purpose-of-business-is-to-create-and-keep-a
21. http://www.forbes.com/sites/stevedenning/2012/04/25/david-brooks-competitiveness-vs-creativity-ge-vs-apple/
22. http://www.forbes.com/sites/stevedenning/2011/11/19/peggy-noonan-on-steve-jobs-and-why-big-companies-die/
23. http://www.gallup.com/poll/165269/worldwide-employees-engaged-work.aspx
24. https://cec.executiveboard.com/public/CEC_Mobilization.pdf
25. Based on empirical research from Stigter, M. (2010) '(DIS) ENGAGEMENT: Critical Drivers and Outcomes as Perceived by Employees', Unpublished PhD Thesis, Lancaster University Management School, Lancaster, UK.
26. http://performance.ey.com/wp-content/uploads/downloads/2014/02/ EY-Performance-Using-social-media1.pdf
27. http://www.deloitte.com/assets/DcomMiddleEast/Local%20 Assets/Documents/Services/Consulting/HC%202014/Lead%20and%20 develop/me_human-capital-2014_quest-workforce-capability.pdf
28. http://www.linkedin.com/today/post/article/20140311001037–131079-are-you-an-overwhelmed-employee-new-research-says-yes
29. Adaptedfrom:http://www.linkedin.com/today/post/article/20140311001037–131079-are-you-an-overwhelmed-employee-new-research-says-yes
30. http://dupress.com/periodical/trends/global-human-capital-trends-2014
31. http://www.linkedin.com/today/post/article/20140311001037–131079-are-you-an-overwhelmed-employee-new-research-says-yes
32. Ibid.
33. Based on empirical research from Stigter, M. (2010) '(DIS) ENGAGEMENT: Critical Drivers and Outcomes as Perceived by Employees', Unpublished PhD Thesis, Lancaster University Management School, Lancaster, UK.
34. http://www.forbes.com/sites/louisefron/2013/08/12/three-reasons-your-best-employees-dont-feel-recognized/
35. Stogdill, R.M. (1974) *Handbook of Leadership: A Survey of Theory and Research*, New York, NY: The Free Press.

36. De Vries, M.K. (2001) *The Leadership Mystique: Leading Behavior in the Human Enterprise*, London, UK: Financial Times/ Prentice Hall.
37. Bacharach, S.B. (2006) *Keep Them on Your Side: Leading and Managing for Momentum*, Avon, MA: Platinum Press.
38. http://d2mtr37y39tpbu.cloudfront.net/wpcontent/uploads/2014/03/GlobalHumanCapitalTrends_2014.pdf
39. Adapted from: http://www.psychologytoday.com/blog/the-end-work-you-know-it/201306/the-golden-rule-leadership
40. http://stevedenning.typepad.com/steve_denning/2011/01/is-the-problem-with-capitalism-that-people-try-to-fix-it.html

2 Strategic Sensing – Not Just Thinking

1. Goldman, E. F. (2012) 'Leadership Practices that Encourage Strategic Thinking', *Journal of Strategy and Management*, 5 (1): 26.
2. Casey, A. and Goldman, E. F. (2010) 'Building a Culture that Encourages Strategic Thinking', *Journal of Leadership & Organizational Studies*, 17 (2): 119.
3. As cited in: Goldman, E. F. (2007) 'Strategic Thinking at the Top', *MIT Sloan Management Review*, 48 (4): 75.
4. Mintzberg, H. (1994) 'The Rise and Fall of Strategic Planning', *Harvard Business Review*, 72: 107–114.
5. As cited in Hoverstadt, P. (2008) *The Fractal Organization: Creating Sustainable Organizations with the Viable System Model*, Chichester: Wiley.
6. http://www.nextbigwhat.com/steve-jobs-quote-on-entrepreneurship-297/
7. Hodgkinson, G.P. Sadler-Smith, E. Burke, L.A., Claxton, G. and Sparrow, P.R. (2009) 'Intuition in Organizations: Implications for Strategic Management, *Long Range Planning*, 42: 277–292.
8. http://www.forbes.com/sites/tanyaprive/2013/05/02/top-32-quotes-every-entrepreneur-should-live-by/
9. http://en.wikiquote.org/wiki/George_Santayana
10. Argyris C (1990) *Overcoming Organizational Defenses: Facilitating Organizational Learning*, Boston: Allyn & Bacon.
11. Senge P, Kleiner A, Roberts C, Ross R (1994) *The Fifth Discipline Fieldbook, Strategies and Tools for Building A Learning Organization*, New York: Doubleday.
12. Taleb, N. N. (2010) *The Black Swan: The Impact of the Highly Improbable*, New York: Randon House.
13. http://en.wikipedia.org/wiki/Robert_Anton_Wilson
14. http://www.axialent.com/uploads/paper
15. http://en.wikipedia.org/wiki/Reality_tunnel
16. Agor, W. H. (1989) 'The Logic of Intuition. How Top Executives Make Important Decisions' in W. H. Agor (Eds.) *Intuition in Organizations: Leading and Managing Productively*, Newsbury Park: Sage Publications. pp. 157–170.

17. Ibid.
18. Allinson, W. C., Chell, E. and Hayes, J. (2000) 'Intuition and Entrepreneurial Behaviour', *European Journal of Work and Organizational Psychology*, 9(1): 31–43.
19. http://www.virgin.com.au/entrepreneur/richard-bransons-top-20-virgin-inspirational-insights
20. Agor, 'The Logic of intuition'.
21. http://www.academia.edu/509612/Entrepreneurial_Intuition_an_empirical_approach
22. Hodgkinson et al., 'Intuition in Organizations'.
23. Adapted from: Mintzberg, H. 1991. 'Strategic Thinking as "Seeing"'. In (1991) Nasi, J. (ed.) *Arenas of Strategic Thinking*, Helsinki, Finland: Foundation for Economic
24. http://www.quotationspage.com/quote/40889.html
25. Collinson, D. L. (2012) 'Prozac Leadership and the Limits of Positive Thinking', *Leadership*, 8 (2): 87–107.
26. http://www.academia.edu/509612/Entrepreneurial_Intuition_an_empirical_approach
27. Hume, D. (1985) *A Treatise of Human Nature*, London: Penguin.

3   Co-Creating a Compelling Story

1. Vuuren, van M. and Elving, W. J. L. (2008) 'Communication, Sensemaking and Change as a Chord of Three Strands: Practical Implications and a Research Agenda for Communicating Organizational Change', *Corporate Communication: An International Journal*, 13 (3): 349–359.
2. Adapted from Meyer, J.P. and Allen, N.J. (1997) *Commitment in the Workplace: Theory, Research, and Application*, Thousand Oaks, CA: Sage: 11.
3. http://www.mckinsey.com/App_Media/Reports/Financial_Services/The_Inconvenient_Truth_About_Change_Management.pdf
4. Ibid.
5. Reissner, S. C. (2011) 'Patterns of Stories of Organisational Change', *Journal of Organizational Change Management*, 24 (5): 593–609.
6. Ibid.
7. Raelin, J. A. (2012) 'Dialogue and Deliberation as Expression of Democratic Leadership in Participatory Organizational Change', *Journal of Organizational Change Management*, 25 (1): 7–23.
8. Oakland, J. S. and Tanner, S. (2007) 'Successful Change Management', *Total Quality Management*, 18 (1–2): 1–19.
9. Raelin, 'Dialogue and Deliberation'.
10. Ibid.
11. National Coalition for Dialogue and Deliberation (2010) adapted from Raelin, J. A. (2012) 'Dialogue and Deliberation as Expression of Democratic Leadership in Participatory Organizational Change, *Journal of Organizational Change Management*, 25 (1): 7–23.

12. Galpin, T. and Whittington, J.L. (2012) 'Sustainability Leadership: From Strategy to Results, *Journal of Business Strategy,* (33) 4: 40–48.
13. Adapted from Galpin, T. and Whittington, J.L. (2012) 'Sustainability Leadership: From Strategy to Results, *Journal of Business Strategy,* (33) 4: 40–48.
14. Adapted from Raelin, 'Dialogue and Deliberation'.
15. Hensmans, M. Johnson, G. and Yip, G. (2013) *Strategic Transformation: Changing while Winning,* London: Palgrave Macmillan.
16. Stigter, M. (2010) '(DIS) ENGAGEMENT: Critical Drivers and Outcomes as Perceived by Employees', *Unpublished PhD Thesis, Lancaster University Management School,* Lancaster, UK.
17. Hensmans et al., *Strategic Transformation.*
18. As cited in: http://www.mckinsey.com/App_Media/Reports/Financial_ Services/The_ Inconvenient_Truth_About_Change_Management.pdf
19. Ganz, M. as cited in Wilson, D.G. (2010) 'Building Bridges for Change: How Leaders enable Collective Change in Organizations', *Development and Learning in Organizations,* 24 (1): 21–23.
20. Bush, G.R. in Kessler, E.H. (ed) (2013) *Encyclopedia of Management Theory,* Sage Publications, accessed: http://www.gervasebushe.ca/the_AI_model.pdf.
21. Ibid.
22. Ganz, M. as cited in Wilson, 'Building Bridges for Change'.
23. Collins, J.C. and Porras, J.L. (1991) 'Organizational Vision and Visionary Organizations', *California Management Review,* Fall 1991: 30–52.
24. Ibid..
25. Gratton, L. (2000) *Living Strategy: Putting People at the Heart of Corporate Purpose,* London: Financial Times, Prentice Hall.
26. Oswald, S.L. Mossholder, K.W. and Harris, S.G. (1994) Vision Salience and Strategic Involvement: Implication for Psychological Attachment to Organization and Job, *Strategic Management Journal,* 15: 477–489.
27. Carland, J.C. and Carland, J.W. (2012) 'A Model of Shared Entrepreneurial Leadership', Academy of Entrepreneurship Journal, (18) 2: 71–81.
28. Collins, J.C. and Porras, J.L. (1991) 'Organizational Vision and Visionary Organizations', *California Management Review,* Fall 1991: 30–52.
29. Ibid.
30. http://www.bbc.co.uk/news/business-16611040
31. http://www.canadianbusiness.com/blogs-and-comment/most-company-mission-statements-are-rubbish-richard-branson/
32. http://www.canadianbusiness.com/blogs-and-comment/most-company-mission-statements-are-rubbish-richard-branson/
33. Kaplan, R. and Norton, D. (2008) *The Execution Premium: Linking Strategy to Operations for Competitive Advantage,* Boston, MA, Harvard Business School Publishing Corporation.
34. https://www.merck.com/about/home.html
35. http://www.ikea.com/ms/en_MY/about_ikea/the_ikea_way/our_business_idea/index.html
36. http://www.canadianbusiness.com/blogs-and-comment/most-company-mission-statements-are-rubbish-richard-branson/

4   Co-Creating Distinctive Strategies

1. Campbell, A. and Alexander, M. (1997) 'What's Wrong with Strategy?', *Harvard Business Review*, Nov-Dec 1997: 42–51.
2. Mankins, M.C. and Steele, R. (2006) 'Stop Making Plans, Start Making Decisions', *Harvard Business Review*, January 2006: 76–84.
3. Bergen, M. and Peteraf, M. A. (2002) 'Competitor Identification and Competitor Analysis: A Broad-Based Managerial Approach', *Managerial and Decision Economics*, 23: 157–169.
4. Dandira, M. (2011) 'Involvement of Implementers: Missing Element in Strategy Formulation', *Business Strategy Series* 12 (1): 30–34.
5. http://blogs.hbr.org/2008/02/making-strategy-development-ma/
6. Cohen and Levinthal (1990); Kogut and Zander (1992), Drucker (1993); Grant (1996); Teece et al (1997) as referred to by Rossi, C. (2011) 'Online Consumer Communities, Collaborative Learning and Innovation', *Measuring Business Excellence*, 15 (3): 46–62. Adapted from Ramaswamy, V. and Ozcan, K. (2013) 'Strategy and Co-Creation Thinking', *Strategy & Leadership*, 41 (6): 5–10.
7. Nadler, D.A. (2004) 'What's the Board's Role in Strategy Development? Engaging the Board in Corporate Strategy', *Strategy & Leadership*, 32 (2): 25–33.
8. Steinberg, R.M. (2012) 'The Board's Critical Role in Strategy Development', www.Complianceweek.com, April 2012: 52–53.
9. Nadler, D.A. (2004) 'What's the Board's Role in Strategy Development? Engaging the Board in Corporate Strategy', *Strategy & Leadership*, 32 (2): 25–33.
10. http://www.mckinsey.com/insights/strategy/tapping_the_strategic_potential_of_boards
11. http://www.corpgov.deloitte.com/binary/com.epicentric.contentman-agement.servlet.ContentDeliveryServlet/USEng/Documents/Board%20 Governance/Tablet_Deloitte%20Board%20Practices%20Report%202012. pdf
12. http://www.tapestrynetworks.com/initiatives/corporate-governance/ north-american-audit-committee-networks/upload/Tapestry_EY_ MWACN_Vantage_Nov12.pdf
13. http://www.mckinsey.com/insights/strategy/tapping_the_strategic_ potential_of_boards
14. http://sloanreview.mit.edu/article/collaborating-with-customer-communities-lessons-from-the-lego-group/
15. http://www.corpgov.deloitte.com/binary/com.epicentric.contentman-agement.servlet.ContentDeliveryServlet/USEng/Documents/Board%20 Governance/Tablet_Deloitte%20Board%20Practices%20Report%202012. pdf
16. Nadler, D.A. (2004) 'What's the Board's Role in Strategy Development?: Engaging the Board in Corporate Strategy', *Strategy & Leadership*, 32 (2): 25–33.

17. Antal, A.B. and Kresbach-Hnath, C. (2002) 'Internal Outsiders Transform Tradition-Bound Organization', *Reflections*, 4 (2): 23–33.
18. Adapted from Bennis, W. (1989) 'Why Leaders Can't Lead' as quoted in Antal, A.B. and Kresbach-Hnath, C. (2002) 'Internal Outsiders Transform Tradition-Bound Organization', *Reflections*, 4 (2): 23–33.
19. www.nextbigwhat.com/steve-jobs-quote-on-entrepreneurship-297/
20. Antal, A.B. and Kresbach-Hnath, C. (2002) 'Internal Outsiders Transform Tradition-Bound Organization', *Reflections*, 4 (2): 23–33.
21. Ramaswamy, V. and Ozcan, K. (2013) 'Strategy and Co-Creation Thinking', *Strategy & Leadership*, 41 (6): 5–10.
22. http://www.goodreads.com/quotes/15297-if-i-had-asked-people-what-they-wanted-they-would
23. As quoted in: http://www.sagepub.com/ellis/SJO%20Readings/Chapter%203%20-%20Zwick,%20Bonsu%20&%20Darmody.pdf
24. McWilliams (2000); Nambisan and Nambisan (2002); Bauer and Grether (2002); Verona and Prandelli (2006); Gibbert et al (2002); Wiertz and de Ruiter (2007) as referred to by Rossi, C. (2011) 'Online Consumer Communities, Collaborative Learning and Innovation', *Measuring Business Excellence*, 15 (3): 46–62.
25. Rossi, C. (2011) 'Online Consumer Communities, Collaborative Learning and Innovation', *Measuring Business Excellence*, 15 (3): 46–62.
26. http://sloanreview.mit.edu/article/collaborating-with-customer-communities-lessons-from-the-lego-group/
27. Ibid.
28. Ibid.
29. Zwick, D,. Bonsu, S.M. and Darmody, A. (2008) 'Putting Consumers to Work: Co-creation and New Marketing Govern-Mentality', *Journal of Consumer Culture*, 8: 163–196.
30. Adapted from Ibid.
31. http://sloanreview.mit.edu/article/collaborating-with-customer-communities-lessons-from-the-lego-group/
32. Johnason, J. and Vahlne, J. (2011) 'Markets as Networks: Implications for Strategy-Making', *Journal of the Academy of Marketing Sciences*, 39: 484–491.
33. Schindehutte, M. and Morris, M. (2009) 'Advancing Strategic Entrepreneurship Research: The Role of Complexity Science in Shifting the Paradigm', *Entrepreneurship Theory and Practice*, January: 241–276.

5 Realizing Distinctive Strategies

1. Martin, R.L. (2010) 'The Execution Trap: Drawing a Line between Strategy and Execution almost guarantees Failure', *Harvard Business Review*, July-August 2010: 64–71.
2. Adapted from Dupuy, F. (2002) *The Chemistry of Change*, Basingstoke: Palgrave Macmillan.

3. Kaplan, N.S. and Norton, D.P. (2006) 'How to Implement a Strategy without Disrupting your Organization', *Harvard Business Review*, March: 101–109.
4. Dupuy, *The Chemistry of Change*.
5. http://hbr.org/2008/06/the-secrets-to-successful-strategy-execution/ar/1
6. http://business.highbeam.com/437437/article-1G1-151959737/ but-can-you- execute-bruce-barlag-says-executing-strategy\
7. Sourced from: Bigler, W.R. (2001) 'The New Science of Strategy Execution: How Incumbents Become Fast, Sleek Wealth Creators', *Strategy Leadership*, 29 March 2001: 29–34; Allio, M.K. (2005) 'A Short, Practical Guide to Implementing Strategy', *Journal of Business Strategy*, 26 (4): 12–21; Speculand, R. (2009) 'Six Necessary Mind Shifts for Implementing Strategy', *Business Strategy Series*, 10 (3): 167–172; Franken, A. et al (2009) 'Executing Strategic Change: Understanding the Critical Management Elements that Lead to Success', *California Management Review*, 51 (3): 49–61.
8. Adapted from: Manning, T. (2012) 'Managing Change in Hard Times', *Industrial and Commercial Training*, 44 (5): 259–267; Spotlight (2010) 'How Hierarchy Can Hurt Strategy Execution', *Harvard Business Review*, July-August 2010: 74–75.
9. Martin, R.L. (2010) 'The Execution Trap: Drawing a Line between Strategy and Execution almost guarantees Failure', *Harvard Business Review*, July-August 2010: 64–71.
10. Spotlight, 'How Hierarchy Can Hurt Strategy Execution'.
11. Martin, 'The Execution Trap'.
12. Cocks, G. (2010) 'Emerging Concepts for Implementing Strategy, *The TQM Journal*, 22 (3): 260–266.
13. Hubbard et al. (1996) as quoted by Cocks, G. (2010) 'Emerging Concepts for Implementing Strategy, *The TQM Journal*, 22 (3): 260–266.
14. Cocks, 'Emerging Concepts for Implementing Strategy'.
15. Turnbull, S. (2001) 'Corporate Ideology – Meanings and Contradictions for Middle Managers', *British Journal of Management*, Vol. 12: 231–242.
16. Ibid.
17. Adapted from Salih, A. and Doll, Y. (2013) 'A Middle Management Perspective on Strategy Implementation', *International Journal of Business and Management*, 8 (22): 32–39.
18. Floyd and Wooldridge (1997) and Balagun (2003) as quoted in Hope, O. (2010) 'The Politics of Middle Management Sensemaking and Sensegiving', *Journal of Change Management*, 10 (2): 195–215.
19. Guth, W.D. and MacMillan, I.C. (1986) 'Strategy Implementation versus Middle Management Self-Interest', *Strategic Management Journal*, 7 (4): 313–327.
20. Mair & Thurner (2008) as quoted in Salih, A. and Doll, Y. (2013) 'A Middle Management Perspective on Strategy Implementation', *International Journal of Business and Management*, 8 (22): 32–39.
21. Guth and MacMillan, 'Strategy Implementation versus Middle Management Self-Interest'.

22. Turnbull, 'Corporate Ideology'.
23. Ibid..
24. Ibid.
25. Adapted from Gioia and Chittipeddi (1991) in Hope, O. (2010) 'The Politics of Middle Management Sensemaking and Sensegiving', *Journal of Change Management*, 10 (2): 195–215.
26. Gioia and Chittipeddi (1991) as quoted in Hope, 'The Politics of Middle Management Sensemaking and Sensegiving'.
27. Hope, 'The Politics of Middle Management Sensemaking and Sensegiving'.
28. Adapted from: Allio, M.K. (2005) 'A Short Practical Guide to Implementing Strategy', *The Journal of Business Strategy*, 26 (4): 12–21.
29. http://www.kotterinternational.com/our-principles/urgency
30. Allio, 'A Short Practical Guide'.
31. http://addicted2success.com/quotes/14-steve-jobs-quotes-that-will-warp-your-mind/
32. http://www.goodreads.com/author/quotes/12008.Peter_F_Drucker
33. Allio, 'A Short Practical Guide'.
34. Liedtka, J. (2006) 'Is Your Strategy A Duck?', *Journal of Business Strategy*, 27 (5): 32–37.
35. Drucker, P. (1967) as referred to in: Bigler, W.R. (2001) 'The New Science of Strategy Execution', *Strategy & Leadership*, 29 (3): 29–34.

6 Overcoming Inertia

1. Based on research by Speculand, R. (2009) 'Six Necessary Mind Shifts for Implementing Strategy', *Business Strategy Series*, 10 (3): 167–172. and Speculand, R. (2006) 'Strategy Implementation: We Got the People Factor Wrong: How to Lead your Saboteurs, Double Agents and Mavericks', *Human Resource Management Digest*, 14 (6): 34–37.
2. http://www.goodreads.com/tag/inertia
3. Based on Allcorn, S. and Godkin, L. (2011) 'Workplace Psychodynamics and the Management of Organizational Inertia', *Competitiveness Review: An International Business Journal*, 21 (1): 89–104; and Godkin, L. and Allcorn, S. (2008) 'Overcoming Organizational Inertia: A Tripartite Model for Achieving Strategic Organizational Change', *Journal of Applied Business and Economics*, 8 (1): 82–95.
4. Adapted from Hedberg and Wolff (2003) in Godkin and Allcorn, 'Overcoming Organizational Inertia'.
5. Kieser et al. (2003), as quoted by: Godkin and Allcorn, 'Overcoming Organizational Inertia'.
6. http://www.goodreads.com/quotes/tag/inertia
7. Hedberg and Wolff (2003) in Godkin and Allcorn, 'Overcoming Organizational Inertia'.
8. Allcorn, S. and Godkin, L. (2011) 'Workplace Psychodynamics and the Management of Organizational Inertia', *Competitiveness Review: An International Business Journal*, 21 (1): 89–104.

9. Based on empirical research from Stigter, M. (2010) '(DIS) ENGAGEMENT: Critical Drivers and Outcomes as Perceived by Employees', Unpublished PhD Thesis, Lancaster University Management School, Lancaster, UK.
10. Kahn, W. (1990) 'Psychological Conditions of Personal Engagement and Disengagement at Work', *Academy of Management Journal*, 33 (4): 692–724.
11. Ibid.
12. Based on empirical research from Stigter, '(DIS) ENGAGEMENT'.
13. Lambert, S.J. (2006) 'Both Art and Science: Employing Organizational Documentation in Workplace-Based Research'. In Pitt-Catsouphes, M., Kossek, E.E., & Sweet, S. (Eds.). *The Work and Family Handbook: Multi-Disciplinary Perspectives, Methods, and Approaches.* (pp.503–525). Mahwah, NJ: Lawrence Erlbaum Associates.
14. Based on empirical research from Stigter, '(DIS) ENGAGEMENT'.
15. Bowles, D. and Cooper. C. (2009) *Employee Morale: Driving Performance in Challenging Times*, Basingstoke, UK: Palgrave Macmillan.
16. Based on empirical research from Stigter, '(DIS) ENGAGEMENT'.
17. Ibid.
18. Ibid.
19. Furnham, A. and Taylor, J. (2004) *The Dark Side of Behaviour at Work: Understanding and Avoiding Employees Leaving, Thieving and Deceiving*, New York: Palgrave Macmillan.
20. Coyle-Sharpio, J. Kessler, I. (2000) 'Consequences of the Psychological Contract for the Employment Relationship: A Large Scale Survey', *Journal of Management Studies* 37 (7): 903–930.
21. Argyris, C. (1960) in Guest, D. (2004) 'The Psychology of the Employment Relationship: An Analysis based on the Psychological Contract', *Applied Psychology: An International Review*, 53 (4): 541–555.
22. Herriot, P. and Pemberton, C. (1997) 'Facilitating New Deals', *Human Resource Management Journal*, 7(1): 45–56.
23. Adapted from Sparrow, P.R. and Cooper, C.L. (2003) *The Employment Relationship: Key Challenges for HR*, Burlington, MA: Butterworth-Heinemann.
24. Based on empirical research from Stigter, '(DIS) ENGAGEMENT'.
25. Guest, D. (2004a) 'The Psychology of the Employment Relationship: An Analysis based on the Psychological Contract', *Applied Psychology: An International Review*, 53 (4): 541–555.
26. Morrison, E. and Robinson, S. (1997) 'When Employees Feel Betrayed: A Model of How the Psychological Contract Violation Develops', *Academy of Management Review*, 22 (1): 226–256.
27. Herriot, P. (2001) *The Employment Relationship: A Psychological Perspective*, Hove, Routledge.
28. Sparrow and Cooper, *The Employment Relationship*.
29. Referred negative attitudinal and behavioural outcomes based on: Pate, J. Martin, G. and McGoldrick, J. (2003) 'The Impact of Psychological Contract Violation on Employee Attitudes and Behaviour', *Employee Relations*, 25 (6):

557–573; Robinson, S. L. and Morrison, E.W. (1995) 'Psychological Contracts and OCB: The Effect of Unfulfilled Obligations on Civic Virtue Behavior', *Journal of Organizational Behavior*, 16: 289–298; Turnley, W. and Feldmann, D. (1999) 'A Discrepancy Model of Psychological Contract Violations', *Human Resource Management Review*, 9 (3): 367–386; Robinson, S. L. & Rousseau, D. M. (1994) 'Violating the Psychological Contract: Not the Exception but the Norm', *Journal of Organizational Behavior*, 15: 245–259.

30. Based on empirical research from Stigter, '(DIS) ENGAGEMENT'.
31. Based on: Turnley, W. and Feldmann, D. (1999) 'A Discrepancy Model of Psychological Contract Violations', *Human Resource Management Review*, 9 (3): 367–386; Marcus, B. and Schuler, H. (2004) 'Antecedents of Counterproductive Behavior at Work: A General Perspective, *Journal of Applied Psychology*, Vol.89, No.4: 647–660; Ackroyd, S. and Thompson, P. (1999) *Organisational Misbehaviour*, London: Sage.
32. Ackroyd, S. and Thompson, P. (1999) *Organisational Misbehaviour*, London: Sage.
33. Marcus, B. and Schuler, H. (2004) 'Antecedents of Counterproductive Behavior at Work: A General Perspective, *Journal of Applied Psychology*, 89 (4): 647–660.
34. Furnham and Taylor, *The Dark Side of Behaviour at Work*.
35. Sackett (2002) as cited in Furnham and Taylor, *The Dark Side of Behaviour at Work*.
36. Based on empirical research from Stigter, '(DIS) ENGAGEMENT'.
37. Based on Allcorn and Godkin, 'Workplace Psychodynamics'; and Kets de Vries, M. and Miller, E. (1984) *The Neurotic Organization*, San Francisco, CA: Jossey-Bass.
38. Adapted from Allcorn and Godkin, 'Workplace Psychodynamics'.
39. Adapted from Diamond (1996) as cited in Allcorn and Godkin, 'Workplace Psychodynamics'.
40. Based on research by: Chartered Institute of Personnel and Development (2006) *Reflections on Employee Engagement: Change Agenda*. London: CIPD; Chartered Institute of Personnel and Development (2006) *Annual Survey 2006: How Engaged Are British Employees*. London: CIPD; Robinson, D. Hooker, H. and Hayday, S. (2007) 'Engagement: The Continuing Story', IES Report 447, Brighton: The Institute for Employment Studies; Vance, R. (2006) *Employee Engagement and Commitment: A Guide to Understanding, Measuring and Increasing Engagement in your Organization*, Alexandria, VA: SHRM Foundation.
41. Based on empirical research from Stigter, '(DIS) ENGAGEMENT'.
42. Weinberg, A.W. and Cooper, C. (2007) 'Surviving the Workplace: A Guide to Emotional Well-being', *Psychology at Work Series*, London: Thomson Learning.
43. Robertson, I. and Tinline, G (2008) 'Understanding and Improving Psychological Well-being for Individual and Organisational Effectiveness' In Kinder, A., Hughes, R. And Cooper, C.L.(2008) *Employee Well-being Support: A Workplace Resource*, Chichester: John Wiley and Sons Ltd.

44. http://cep.lse.ac.uk/seminarpapers/WB-01–06–11ROBERTSON.pdf
45. Kahn, 'Psychological Conditions of Personal Engagement'.
46. Based on empirical research from Stigter, '(DIS) ENGAGEMENT'.
47. Ibid.
48. Bourcier and Palobart (2008) in Brun, J. and Dugas, N. (2008) 'An Analysis of Employee Recognition: Perspectives on Human Resources Practices', *The International Journal of Human Resource Management*, 19 (4): 716–730.
49. Brun, J. and Dugas, N. (2008) 'An Analysis of Employee Recognition: Perspectives on Human Resources Practices', *The International Journal of Human Resource Management*, 19 (4): 716–730.
50. http://www.cgsst.com/eng/expression/eight-quality-criteria.asp
51. Furnham and Taylor, *The Dark Side of Behaviour at Work*.
52. http://www.cgsst.com/eng/expression/eight-quality-criteria.asp
53. Saunderson, R. (2004) 'Survey Findings of the Effectiveness of Employee Recognition in the Public Sector', *Public Personnel Management*, 33 (3): 255–275.
54. Furnham and Taylor, *The Dark Side of Behaviour at Work*.
55. Based on Furnham and Taylor, *The Dark Side of Behaviour at Work*; and on empirical research from Stigter, '(DIS) ENGAGEMENT'.
56. Based on: Rodwell, J.J. Noblet, A. Stean, P. Osborne, S. Allisey, A. (2009) 'Investigating People Management Issues in a Third Sector Health Care Organisation: An Inductive Approach', *Australian Journal of Advanced Nursing*, 22(2): 55–62; and Furnham and Taylor, *The Dark Side of Behaviour at Work*.
57. Saunderson, R. (2004) 'Survey Findings of the Effectiveness of Employee Recognition in the Public Sector', *Public Personnel Management*, 33(3): 255–275.
58. http://www.cgsst.com/eng/definition/a-profile-of-employee-recognition.asp.
59. Ibid. and Brun, J. and Dugas, N. (2008) 'An Analysis of Employee Recognition: Perspectives on Human Resources Practices', *The International Journal of Human Resource Management*, 19(4): 716–730.
60. Brun and Dugas, 'An Analysis of Employee Recognition'.
61. Saunderson, 'Survey Findings'.
62. Based on empirical research from Stigter, '(DIS) ENGAGEMENT'.
63. Brun and Dugas, 'An Analysis of Employee Recognition'.
64. Bourcier & Palobart (1997) as cited in: http://www.cgsst.com/eng/resources-reconnaissance-travail/bibliographies-reconnaissance-travail.asp
65. Based on empirical research from Stigter, '(DIS) ENGAGEMENT'; and Brun and Dugas: http://www.cgsst.com/eng/definition/eight-subcategories-of-employee-recognition.asp
66. Saunderson, 'Survey Findings'.
67. Furnham and Taylor, *The Dark Side of Behaviour at Work*.

7 Sustaining Organizational Energy

1. http://www.ccocouncil.org/site/defining-the-cco.aspx
2. http://blogs.hbr.org/2011/04/the-rise-of-the-chief-customer/
3. http://www.forbes.com/2011/02/10/chief-customer-officer-leadership-cmo-network-rise.html
4. http://blogs.hbr.org/2011/04/the-rise-of-the-chief-customer/
5. http://www.ccocouncil.org/site/the-role-of-the-cco.aspx
6. http://blogs.hbr.org/2011/04/the-rise-of-the-chief-customer/
7. http://www.forbes.com/2011/02/10/chief-customer-officer-leadership-cmo-network-rise.html
8. Adapted from: http://en.wikipedia.org/wiki/Critical_mass_(sociodynamics)
9. Bruch, H. and Vogel, B. (2011) *Fully Charged: How Great Leaders Boost Their Organisation's Energy and Ignite High Performance*, Boston: Harvard Business Review Press.
10. http://www.henley.ac.uk/web/FILES/corporate/clWhite_Paper_Leadership_to_boost_your_organisations_energy_and_performance_by_Dr_Bernd_Vogel_v2. pdf
11. Ibid.
12. Ibid.
13. Bacharach, S.B. (2006) *Keep Them on Your Side*, Avon, MA: Platinum Press.
14. http://www.sail-world.com/USA/Americas-Cup:Gary-Jobson-goes-One-on-One-with-Jimmy-Spithill/118308
15. http://en.wikipedia.org/wiki/Force
16. http://breakingmuscle.com/sports-psychology/momentum-recognizing-and-dealing-with-it
17. http://performance.ey.com/2014/02/20/using-social-media-engage-workforce/
18. Ibid.
19. http://www.deloitte.com/assets/DcomAustralia/Local%20Assets/Documents/Services/Consulting/Human%20Capital/GlobalHumanCapitalTrends_2014.pdf
20. http://performance.ey.com/2014/02/20/using-social-media-engage-workforce/
21. http://www.albert-einstein-quotes.org.za/all-einstein-quotes/and-more-einstein
22. http://www.scribd.com/doc/6745553/Jack-Welch-Straight-From-the-Gut

Index

Printed and bound by CPI Group (UK) Ltd, Croydon, CR0 4YY